Senior High Workbook
Cycle B

Eleanor Suther, OSB
Jeanita F. Strathman Lapa

Contributing Authors

Genevieve Cuny, OSF

Mary Fox, OP

Kate Kuenstler, PHJC

Betty McCafferty, CSJ

Kay Morissey

Doris Murphy

Judy Yunker, OSB

BROWN ROA
Publishing Media

Dubuque, Iowa

Nihil Obstat
Rev. Richard L. Schaefer

Imprimatur
✠Most Rev. Daniel W. Kucera, O.S.B.
Archbishop of Dubuque
December 4, 1989

The Imprimatur is an official declaration that a book or pamphlet is free
of doctrinal or moral error. No implication is contained therein that
anyone who granted the Imprimatur agrees with the contents, opinions,
or statements expressed.

Acknowledgments

The development of this series was partially funded by:

The Catholic Church Extension Society, Chicago, IL

The Catholic Communications Campaign, New York, NY

Mount Saint Scholastica Convent, Atchison, KS

Archbishop's Fund for Sisters, Los Angeles, CA

St. Joseph Foundation, Concordia, KS

Social Justice Fund, Conventual Franciscan Friars, Midwest Province

and by smaller donations from over thirty bishops, dioceses, and religious communities who serve in small
town and country parishes.

Book Team

Publisher—Ernest T. Nedder
Editorial Director—Sandra Hirstein
Production Editor—Marilyn Bowers Gorun
Production Manager—Marilyn Rothenberger
Interior Design—Debra L. O'Brien, Cathy A. Frantz
Cover Design—Cathy A. Frantz
Cover Illustrations—Stanley J. Lapa, Jr., Judith McCully
Interior Activity Illustrations—Mary Fahey
Sunday Thematic Illustrations—Stanley J. Lapa, Jr., Judith McCully,
Jane Stembridge, Cathy A. Frantz

Photo Credits

Bob Coyle—16, 91; Editorial Development Associates—8, 44, 48, 84,
123 right; Robert Fried—22, 114, 123 left; Maryknoll—100; Mary E.
Messenger—24; Chip and Rosa Maria Peterson—68, 71, 107; Robert
Roethig—18, 35, 59, 62, 66, 76, 104; James L. Shaffer—2, 12, 32, 34,
40, 42, 57, 74, 80, 81, 89, 98, 110, 120; Ulrike Welsch—21, 52; Jim
Whitmer—90

ISBN 0-697-2892-5

10 9 8 7 6 5 4 3 2

Contents

First Sunday of
Advent

Waiting on God

Readings: Isaiah 63:16-17, 19, 64:2-7; 1 Corinthians 1:3-9; Mark 13:33-37

The Liturgical Year I

Everyone has certain days of the year which stand out for them. Some days are celebrations of events that have happened and which we want to remember. We celebrate those events each year on that date. Name some dates that are important for you and your family:

Date

Why it is important

e.g. Jan 29

My parent's wedding anniversary—the beginning of our family's life together.

1. _____

2. _____

3. _____

4. _____

Telling stories is an important part of the celebration of these important events in our lives. In a way, they help tell the story of our lives. Each of us has our own stories, and we have stories we share with others, such as our family stories. Sometimes our extended family gathers for a reunion, and we hear parts of the family stories we had never heard before. Older members of the family often have stories to tell us of our grandparents, great-grandparents, and other relatives in the past. But we also hear stories about events in the lives of family members which occurred since we last met. Our own stories become part of the whole family's story, too.

Our community has a story, too, and certain events are important for the community to celebrate. So it is with our country and our Church, and all the communities to which we belong.

The Church is a community formed by a story, a story of the God who loves us and who sent His Son to redeem us. That story becomes our story when we are adopted into God's family, the Church, at baptism. Catholics celebrate God's story every week when we read parts of God's story from the Bible. We also celebrate parts of God's story in special celebrations such as Easter and Christmas. But these are not just celebrations of past events. These celebrations help us to enter more deeply into the story, into the mystery of our life with God. We call this year-long celebration of the Christian mystery the *liturgical year.*

Advent

The liturgical year begins with the season of Advent. Advent is a time of preparation for the celebration of the coming of Jesus. Jesus came in history almost two thousand years ago. We await Jesus' coming at the end of history and at the end of our own personal history, at the time of our death. But Jesus also comes into our lives in the present, in a thousand different ways: through the sacraments, through the reading of Scripture, in prayer, in the gathering of Christians, through the ministry of other people.

Advent is a time to renew our relationship with God. It is a time to be quiet and look for all the ways God comes into our lives. It is a time to recapture our vision of what it means to be a Christian.

Reread the Scripture readings for the First Sunday of Advent. Write down two phrases from each reading which will help you to recapture the vision of what it means to be a Christian.

Isaiah 63:16-17, 19, 64:2-7

- _____
- _____

1 Corinthians 1:3-9

- _____
- _____

Mark 13:33-37

- _____
- _____

Look up the following information in an encyclopedia, and report to your family what you have learned.

Why do Christians celebrate Christmas on December 25?

What is meant by the twelve days of Christmas?

What celebrations have traditionally been part of these twelve days?

Second Sunday of
Advent

Prepare the Way of the Lord

Readings: Isaiah 40:1–5, 9–11; 2 Peter 3:8–14; Mark 1:1–8

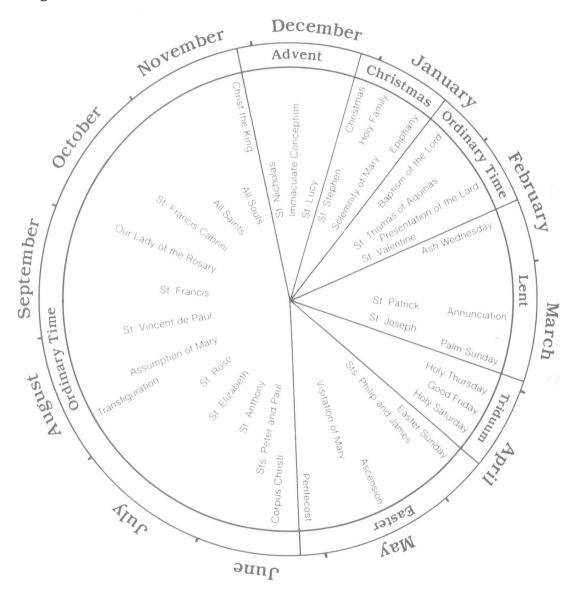

The Liturgical Year II

The most important event in the liturgical year, the one that makes sense of all the others is the death and resurrection of Jesus. We celebrate this event in the Easter Triduum. The word *triduum* is Latin for three days. The celebration begins with the evening Mass of the Lord's Supper on Thursday and ends with Easter Sunday. We prepare for this season by observing forty days of preparation called Lent. After the celebration of the Easter Triduum, we celebrate the resurrection during the fifty days of Easter which end with Pentecost. On Pentecost we celebrate the gift of the Holy Spirit to the Church.

Another focus of the liturgical year is the celebration of the incarnation, the birth of the Son of God as one of us. The celebration of Christmas stretches out to several weeks as we ponder different aspects of the wonder of the incarnation. We end our Christmas celebration with the celebration of the baptism of Jesus. We prepare for the celebration of Christmas during the season of Advent. Between Christmastide and the beginning of Lent and between Pentecost and Advent we celebrate Ordinary Time. On these Sundays we hear readings from the Scriptures which help us ponder the mystery of God's life with us every day.

The liturgical year begins each year with the First Sunday of Advent. The date of Easter varies each year because it is determined by the vernal equinox. Using a calendar for the coming year, indicate the dates on which we will celebrate the following. Remember, the liturgical year begins with Advent of this year.

Date	Event
_____	First Sunday of Advent
_____	Easter Sunday
_____	Ash Wednesday
_____	Pentecost
_____ to _____	Advent
_____ to _____	Christmastide
_____ to _____	Lent
_____ to _____	Easter Triduum
_____ to _____	Easter time
_____ to _____	Ordinary time

Look up the following information in an encyclopedia. Share your information with your family.

1. Orthodox Christians celebrate Easter on a different date than do Western Christians. What is the reason for the difference? How does each group determine when the Easter Triduum will be celebrated?

2. What are the major celebrations in the Jewish year? Are there any similarities between Christian celebrations and Jewish celebrations? What celebrations are part of the Moslem religion? What similarities do you see between these celebrations and Christian celebrations? Do any religions observe a season similar to Advent?

The Precursor

Readings: **Isaiah 61:1-2, 10-11; 1 Thessalonians 5:16-24; John 1:6-8, 19-28**

Advent is a time to renew our understanding of what it means to be Christian. We tell the stories about the people who waited for so long for the coming of the Messiah. We look forward to the celebration of Christmas when we will tell the stories of the birth of Jesus. We reflect on what it means that Jesus will come again. We remember that Jesus has died and risen for our salvation. He gives us the power of his Spirit to carry on his mission.

Read Isaiah 61:1-2; 10-11. Chapters 56-66 of the Book of Isaiah were probably written after the exiles returned to Jerusalem. Scholars call this part Trito-Isaiah (Third Isaiah). The prophet was disappointed about the way the return had turned out. He proclaimed a time in the future when God's reign would surely come. Jesus quoted this passage to explain what he was doing. **Read Luke 4:17-21.** How does the passage from Isaiah describe the work of Jesus? Give two examples from Jesus' life.

1. _____

_____

2. _____

_____

Jesus gave the Church the mission of continuing his work on earth. How does the passage from Isaiah describe the work of the Church? Finish these sentences.

1. The Church brings glad tidings to the lowly by _____

_____

2. The Church heals the brokenhearted by _____

_____

3. The Church proclaims liberty to captives by _____

_____

Like Jesus, the Church and its members are called to serve, rather than to be served. Our task is to cooperate with the coming of God's reign on earth. Like Jesus who went about doing good, we are called to heal the sick and reconcile people with one another and with God. Christians work with many others to help relieve the lot of the poor and the oppressed.

The kingdom of God is not just a worldly paradise. As Christians we know that God's reign of justice and peace will never be completely realized until the end of time. But we also know that God's power in us can do more than we realize or even imagine. As Christians we cooperate with God's power so that God's reign is established in every person's heart and, through them, in the whole world.

For many people, the celebration of Christmas is simply a secular holiday of gift giving and partying. They forget or do not know the real meaning of Christmas. Like John the Baptist, our task is to point out Jesus. What are ways you could help others see Christ in the Christmas season?

_____ Organize a group to sing Christmas carols for the elderly and shut-ins.

_____ Ask your family to work with you to adopt a poor family for Christmas.

_____ Help an elderly or disabled neighbor to winterize his or her home.

_____ Offer to babysit with the younger children while your parents do Christmas shopping.

_____ Befriend a lonely student at school.

_____ Forgive someone who has hurt you.

_____ Write a letter of comfort to someone who is sad or brokenhearted.

_____ Help to free someone who is a "captive" through addiction to alcohol, tobacco, or other drugs.

Name something else you could do.

_____

_____

Tell how someone has made Christ visible for you this week.

_____

_____

_____

_____

Decide which one of the ways of making Christ visible you will choose to do. Write your plans for doing that here.

_____

_____

_____

_____

_____

_____

_____

_____

_____

_____

_____

_____

_____

_____

Saying Yes to God

Readings: 2 Samuel 7:1–5, 8–11, 16; Romans 16:25–27; Luke 1:26–38

Christians honor Mary as especially "blessed among women." But Mary is blessed not just because she is the mother of the Savior. Mary is blessed because she always listened to God's word and lived it out. We look to Mary as a model for all Christians.

When God's messenger told Mary that she was chosen by God to be the mother of His Son, Mary did not know what that would mean. But she said "Yes" because she trusted God completely. All through her life Mary continued to trust God. When she didn't completely understand what had happened, she continued to reflect on the events in her heart.

For centuries, Catholic Christians have used the rosary to reflect with Mary on the mysteries (events) of faith. The rosary uses a repetitive prayer to help focus our minds on the mysteries. Each part or decade begins with the Lord's Prayer and ends with the Glory to the Father. In between are ten Hail Marys.

As we say the prayers we focus our attention on one of the joyful, sorrowful, or glorious mysteries of our faith. We think about how Mary would have responded in that situation. We think about times we have been in similar situations. We think about how we can live as faithful loving Christians.

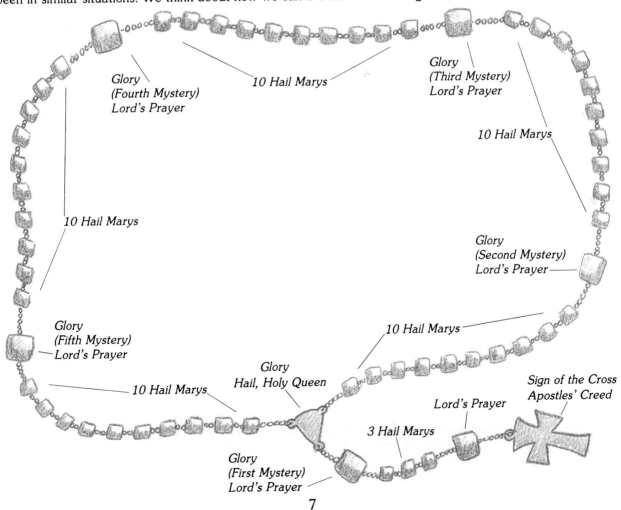

Glory
(Fourth Mystery)
Lord's Prayer

10 Hail Marys

Glory
(Third Mystery)
Lord's Prayer

10 Hail Marys

10 Hail Marys

Glory
(Second Mystery)
Lord's Prayer

Glory
(Fifth Mystery)
Lord's Prayer

10 Hail Marys

Glory
Hail, Holy Queen

Sign of the Cross
Apostles' Creed

Lord's Prayer

3 Hail Marys

Glory
(First Mystery)
Lord's Prayer

Some people think the rosary is very easy to pray. That is not necessarily true. Of course, anyone can say the prayers and use the beads of the rosary. But that is not how the rosary is meant to be used. It takes a lot of practice to learn to pray the rosary in a way that helps one to grow in understanding the mysteries of our faith through contemplation.

Sometimes it is helpful to read from the Bible the story of the mystery we are contemplating. Then we can think about what we have read while we say the ten Hail Marys of that decade. Or we can read one verse from the Bible story before each Hail Mary.

Listed below are the Joyful Mysteries of the Rosary. Use your Bible to find and read the stories of these mysteries. Write the chapter and verse of the story in the Bible.

The Joyful Mysteries

1. The Annunciation: The angel tells Mary she will be the mother of the Savior.

   Luke _____ : _____
       chapter   verses

2. The Visitation: Mary visits her cousin Elizabeth.

   Luke _____ : _____
       chapter   verses

3. The Birth of Jesus

   Luke _____ : _____
       chapter   verses

   Matthew _____ : _____
       chapter   verses

4. The Presentation of Jesus in the Temple

   Luke _____ : _____
       chapter   verses

5. The Finding of the Child Jesus in the Temple

   Luke _____ : _____
       chapter   verses

Choose one of the joyful mysteries. Write a paragraph telling how you think Mary felt in that situation. Of what situation in your life does this remind you? What does this mystery teach you about how to live your life?

_____

_____

_____

_____

_____

The Family of Jesus

Readings: **Sirach 3:2-6, 12-14; Colossians 3:12-21; Luke 2:22-40**

An important task of your teenage years is a task for both teenagers and their parents. Perhaps you can remember a time in your life when you thought your parents could do no wrong. That is a normal attitude for a little child. Parents help to make our childhood world secure. When we begin to realize that our parents are real people and make mistakes, even bad ones, it is often hard to take. Sometimes we expect our parents to be perfect, and so we are angry when we discover that they are not.

Your teenage years are a time to begin to establish a new relationship with your parents. Your parents are still there for you. They still help to make your world secure. But you probably find that you now have more of a desire to be independent. You are beginning the task of separating from your parents, which is such an important part of becoming an adult. Now your parents' task involves helping you to learn to stand on your own, to learn to use your freedom responsibly, to grow into the wonderful and unique person God has created you to be.

It can be a difficult task for parents to know when to let you stand on your own and when to offer you the strong support of rules, guidelines, and expectations. Sometimes, in order to help you to develop your inner strength, they will need to enforce their rules with sanctions. In this task, both parents and teens make mistakes. There can be anger, hurt feelings, and arguments. Both parents and teens need love, patience, and forgiveness in order to accomplish this task. Communication, talking things over, can be an important part of cooperating in establishing this new relationship.

Honoring your parents at this stage means something different than it did when you were seven or ten years old. Now you need to learn to communicate with your parents in a new way. An important step in communication is coming to know your parents as the unique persons they are. This involves listening and sharing on the part of both parents and children. It involves coming to understand each other's goals, concerns, preferences, and problems.

Have you ever asked your parents about their childhood or teenage experiences? What did they enjoy doing when they were your age? Who were their favorite musicians or athletes? What were the hardest issues for them to work out with their parents as they grew up?

When was the last time you had a real conversation with your parents about something that was important to you? What are the concerns which cause the most tension between you and your parents? When your parents were young did they have tension over these issues with their parents? How did they resolve the issues? In what way is the world in which you live different from your parents' teenage world? What can you learn from them?

As long as there are parents and children, there will be tension as parents and teens work out their new relationship. The author of the book of Sirach had advice for young people of his day. **Read Sirach 3: 2-14.** Is Sirach's advice still useful for young people today? Explain.

_____

_____

_____

_____

9

Communications Skills

A good conversation with your parents can help both you and your parents to recognize the love that unites you. It can help you to know that your parents really do support you and that they want what is best for you. It can help your parents to know that you really do respect them and are grateful for what they have done for you. Some rules for communication can help you to have a good conversation with your parents.

1. Be respectful in the way you talk with your parents. Nothing stops communication faster than a sarcastic remark, an angry retort, or an offensive tone of voice. Speaking respectfully to your parents will help them to speak respectfully to you.

2. Tell how you feel. Don't make accusations. Instead of saying, "You never listen to me," try saying, "I don't quite know how to explain this. Can you help me?" Use "I messages" rather than "you messages." "I can't find my socks," instead of, "What did you do with my socks?"

3. When someone is talking to you, stop and listen to them. Stop and pay attention. If you respect the other person in this way, the other person can be more clear and respectful of you.

4. Don't let little problems build up. Sometimes people are like balloons. They keep adding little bits of pressure, until the pressure becomes too much. Then they explode over something little. The other person finds this confusing. When something is bothering you, stop and ask the person to talk it over with you. You can say, "I'm kind of upset about something. Do you have time to talk about it now?"

5. Let your parents know you love them. Give them a hug or another sign of affection regularly. It will help them to know even in difficult times that you do love them.

6. When there is something important you want to talk about with your parents, be sure there is plenty of time to talk. Wait until a time when your anger or your parent's anger has cooled down a bit. Pray to the Holy Spirit for guidance for yourself and for your parents.

7. Begin by saying something positive about your parents. If your parents become angry because of what you say, try to understand their anger. Perhaps they are feeling hurt or frightened. Acknowledge their anger. Say something like, "I didn't know you had such strong feelings about this. . . ."

8. Stick to the topic. Don't bring up old hurts or problems.

9. Don't close the conversation because one person gets angry. Anger can be a positive emotion. It helps us know what is important to us. It can be a clue to a solution to our problem. Try to keep the conversation open, even if you end up disagreeing.

10. One's initial feeling of anger is not a sin. It depends on what we do with our anger. The sin comes in nursing our anger, in not forgiving, in retaliating, or in intentionally hurting the other person. It is important to be open to forgiving the other person.

Not all marriages are happy marriages and not all families are happy families. Sometimes families become dysfunctional because of alcoholism or drug dependency or other unresolved problems of one or more family members. Sometimes conflict between the couple becomes so great that they decide to divorce. This is a difficult time for the whole family. Children of dysfunctional families especially need the support of other significant family members or other adults to help them through this situation. It is important for the child to realize that the problem does not mean that he or she is a bad person nor that he or she is the cause of the problem.

Christmastide

Readings: Isaiah 60:1-6; Ephesians 3:2-3, 5-6; Matthew 2:1-12

Most people today do not take astrology very seriously. If we read our horoscope in the daily paper, it is simply for the sake of entertainment. Horoscopes, signs of the zodiac, fortune cookies, no longer have the power for us that they did for people of another time.

The magi in today's gospel story did take astrology seriously. Historically the magi were a highly esteemed class of priestly scholars in Persia. They were Zoroastrians, for whom the movements of the stars predicted earthly activities. They believed that each person on earth was represented by his or her own star in the sky. They reported that they had seen Jesus' star, a sign that this child was a newborn king.

Christian imagination has been very free with the story of the coming of the magi, also called the wise men or the three kings. The gospel does not tell us how many astrologers there were, and Christian artists have painted the picture with as few as two or as many as twelve. Generally the stories have settled on three, although the only historical foundation for that is the three gifts they brought. Some have used Psalm 68:31-32 to speculate that the magi represented the different races. Legend has also attributed names to the "three" kings: Casper, Melchior, and Balthasar. The twentieth century opera, *Amahl and the Night Visitors,* and the carol, "We Three Kings," have helped to fix those names in our memories. We usually add the "three kings" to our crèche, even though the gospel clearly states that by this time the Child Jesus and his mother were to be found in a house in Bethlehem.

We may wonder why the Jewish people were so slow to recognize Jesus as the Messiah if such remarkable events marked his birth and early childhood. It is important to recognize that these stories are more than just an account of the way things happened. They are stories which tell us much more about the meaning of who this child is and what his meaning is for us.

These stories were told by Christian believers after the resurrection of Jesus. Like commentators at the Olympics who tell us about the significant events in the early life of an athlete, these storytellers tell us the significance of what may have seemed to many to be an ordinary event. They may emphasize some aspects of the event and underplay other aspects in order to make their point. So, when we approach this event, the question, "Did this really happen this way?" may not be very helpful. Rather we need to ask, "What does this event reveal to us about God?"

The story as it is told in the Gospel of Matthew is full of symbolism. The magi represent the Gentiles, the non-Jews. Their appearance early in the Gospel emphasizes the fact that Jesus came not only for the Jews, but for all people. The gifts presented by the magi are significant. Gold signifies that the child is a king. Frankincense is a sign of worship and suggests his divinity. Myrrh is an ointment used for burial, a sign that he will die some day. The child and his parents flee to Egypt to escape the cruel Herod. Like Moses, the infant Jesus is saved from death. Like the Israelites, Jesus comes out of Egypt.

The birth of Jesus was announced to the poor shepherds who came to worship the child. But Herod and his advisers do not recognize him. It is only the foreigners and the poor that were able to recognize him. In the end, Jesus was rejected by some religious and political leaders in Israel. But a group of astrologers who did not even recognize the one God of Israel came to worship the Child.

What can the story mean for us today? Can we be too secure in our faith? Are there ways in which we have failed to recognize where God is being revealed today? A faithful Jew would never have expected a Zoroastrian to recognize the Messiah. Are there ways God is manifesting Himself to us today in unexpected ways?

11

The Christian Science Monitor carried this comment of Gerda Weissmann Klein, a survivor of the Holocaust.

Most people think the Holocaust camps were like snake pits—that people stepped on each other for survival. It wasn't like that at all. There was kindness, support, understanding.

I often talk about a childhood friend of mine, Ilse. She once found a raspberry in the camp and carried it in her pocket all day to present to me that night on a leaf.

Imagine a world in which your entire possession is one raspberry, and you give it to a friend. Those are the moments I want to remember. People behaved nobly under unspeakable circumstance.

As printed in Reader's Digest *(January 1989): 141.*

Tell a story about a time when you found God manifested in a person or place you least expected.

_____

_____

_____

_____

_____

_____

_____

_____

_____

_____

_____

_____

_____

_____

_____

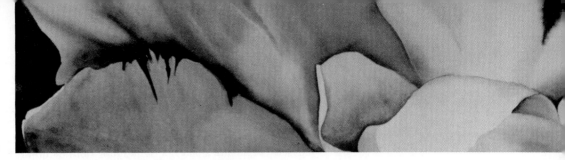

Here Is My Chosen One

Readings: **Isaiah 42:1–4, 6–7; Acts 10:34–38; Mark 1:7–11**

When you were baptized, you were given a name. Do you know why your parents gave you your name? Some parents give their children names of favorite friends or relatives. Others choose the name of a famous person they hope their child will imitate. Christians have often given their children biblical or saints' names.

Among the Lakota Indians of southcentral South Dakota, there is a name-giving ceremony which traditionally took place when a child was three years old. Until that time the child was called *Winyan* if she was a girl or *Wicasa* if he was a boy. For three years the parents observed the spirit of the child. When the child became three years old, a certain uncle or aunt would name the child. The name given signified the spirit living in the child and his or her gift to the tribal community. The naming set the individual apart for a spiritual destiny.

Today many Lakota families who are Christian name their children at birth or at the time of the baptism of the child. Often they use Indian names which signify the spirit of the child.

Answer these questions.

What is the meaning or significance of your name?

_____

_____

_____

Are you named after someone special? Whom?

_____

_____

What do you know about your patron saint?

_____

_____

_____

_____

As you think about the gifts you have discovered in yourself, what work do you think God is calling you to do?

_____

_____

_____

_____

_____

Long before your birth, you were chosen by God. You were chosen to be committed to the mission of Jesus Christ to bring the good news of God's love to every human being. You were called not only to spread the reign of God, but also to enjoy it forever with God in heaven.

You were initiated into this mission at your baptism. You were given the power of the Holy Spirit to guide and strengthen you. Your parents and godparents promised to bring you up as a good Christian. At your confirmation, you take upon yourself the responsibility of living your faith as an adult member of the Church. As an adult member of the community, you will realize that it is only the Spirit of Jesus which can bring success to your mission of spreading the good news of God's kingdom.

At confirmation some Christians take a new name. They choose the name of a saint or a biblical character they admire and want to imitate. If you were to choose a new name, what name would you choose? Why?

_____

_____

_____

_____

Sometimes when we think about spreading the good news of God's kingdom, we think of major decisions, like joining the Peace Corps or becoming a priest. Your mission of spreading the kingdom is, of course, the major consideration when you are thinking about choosing your life's work or making other major commitments.

But the work of spreading the kingdom takes place in your everyday world right now also. Learning to work with others at school or on a team, being considerate of the members of your family, studying to prepare yourself for your life work, are all ways that you are working to spread the kingdom right now.

On the calendar below, write down the major activities that occupied your days this past week.

Sunday	Monday	Tuesday	Wednesday	Thursday	Friday	Saturday

Choose one of the activities and tell how you were working to spread the kingdom of God.

_____

_____

_____

_____

14

Second Sunday in
Ordinary Time

God Calls— I Respond

Readings: 1 Samuel 3:3-10, 19; 1 Corinthians 6:13-15, 17-20; John 1:35-42

One of the most powerful signs of your growth into adulthood is the feelings you experience regarding persons of the other sex. Sex is God's way of enabling men and women to be His partners in creating another human being. Your growth to adulthood is not without purpose. God has not created you to be an adult just to be an adult. He has created you to be His partner in creation. In fact, God wants you to grow into responsible adulthood, not only to continue His creation of other human beings, but to continue His creation of the world.

Read 1 Corinthians 6:13-20.

What problems did Paul see in the community at Corinth?

_____

_____

What standards did Paul propose to them?

_____

_____

What reasons did Paul give them for these standards?

_____

_____

The Church's View of Sex

Perhaps the greatest personal adjustment you will face as you grow to maturity is in regard to the growing demands of your sexual nature. The world around you, your own age group, and the demands of your maturing body will focus your attention on sex and sexuality.

Because the ideas, feelings, desires, and bodily drives you will increasingly experience will put more and more pressure on you to respond to sexual urges, it is important to continue to develop a healthy attitude toward sex in your own life. The Church can help you handle the demands of your sexual nature because it presents a balanced view of sex based on religious values.

The Church views sexual expression as normal, healthy, natural, good, and holy in marriage when it promotes the good of the individuals and of the couple and conforms to God's plan for the use of sex. The Church teaches that sex is designed by God for having children. Thus the intimate expressions of sex should take place in a family circumstance: a husband and a wife expressing their love for each other in an intense, intimate, and creative way.

As far as young people are concerned, the Church teaches that the intimate expressions of sex outside of marriage are morally wrong. Young people are neither ready for nor capable of handling the responsibilities of sex. They are neither old enough to understand its mystery, experienced enough to start and maintain a family, nor capable of properly caring for children.

The Church's view of sex opposes the common view of sex held by many people in society, including some boys and girls your age. But the Church's view of sex is Christ's view. It is based on Jesus' constant preaching of the respect that people should have for each other. It teaches that men should view with awe and respect a woman's role in God's creative plan, and that women should hold in high regard a man's creative power.

If a human being is the greatest act of God's creation, the power to create that human being (which is what sex is) is a person's greatest human power. It ought to be treated as such.

It is because the Church understands the personal and social pressures of sex that it tries to keep its members aware of the fact that sex is a precious gift from God. It is especially concerned that young people keep sex in its proper perspective in relationship to their total human development. The Church knows that, if they do, they will grow to maturity managing their sexual growth and their sexual appetites to their own good. If they do not, the Church knows, sexual problems may overwhelm them.

1. On what is the Church's view of sex based?

_____

_____

2. Why does the Church insist that sexual intimacy outside of marriage is morally wrong?

_____

_____

Integrating your sexuality is a major task of your adolescent years. From time to time, as you experience different situations, you may need to talk some things over with your parents or another adult you trust. In the meantime it is important to keep the lines of communication open.

Name two things your parents could do that would make it easier for you to talk to them.

_____

_____

Name two things your parents could do that would make it more difficult for you to talk to them.

_____

_____

Name two things that you could do that would make it more difficult for your parents to talk to you.

_____

_____

Sometime in the near future share your answers to these questions with your parents or another adult you trust.

Adapted from Focus on Growth in the Church *(Dubuque, IA: BROWN Publishing–ROA Media, 1985), 104–105.*

Third Sunday in
Ordinary Time

Faith in Jesus Changes Our Lives

Readings: **Jonah 3:1–5, 10; 1 Corinthians 7:29–31; Mark 1:14–20**

Teach me your ways, O Lord. (Psalm 25)

St. Paul established the community of believers in Corinth about the year 50 on his second missionary journey. This community of believers was surrounded by pagan people (people who did not believe in God and the way of living that Jesus taught). Corinth was known for its sinfulness, similar to Nineveh where Jonah was sent by God. This first community of believers at Corinth needed to be reminded of Jesus' way to live. Paul wrote letters to help them remember.

What is the name of the Church, the community of believers to which you belong?

_____

How did you become a member of this community of believers?

_____

As a community of believers we say this anamnesis at Mass:

Christ has died,
Christ is risen,
Christ will come again.

What does each phrase mean to you?

Christ has died _____

_____

Christ is risen _____

_____

Christ will come again _____

_____

Name some ways your faith community is reminded of Jesus' way to live.

_____

_____

_____

You, like St. Paul, have received a call from God. You are called to seek Jesus, to know Jesus, to become holy. You began to answer that call at your baptism. Write a paragraph about your faith journey of following Jesus' way.

_____

_____

_____

_____

_____

Are you satisfied with the way your faith journey is going? Why or why not?

_____

_____

_____

Take a few moments to think about Francis of Assisi. He was called by God to seek Jesus, to know Jesus, to become holy. Francis asked the Lord for guidance.

Prayer of St. Francis

Lord, make me an instrument of your peace.
Where there is hatred, let me sow love,
Where there is injury, pardon,
Where there is doubt, faith,
Where there is despair, hope,
Where there is darkness, light,
Where there is sadness, joy.

O Divine Master, grant that I may not so much seek
To be consoled as to console,
To be understood as to understand,
To be loved as to love.

For it is in giving that we receive.
It is in pardoning that we are pardoned.
And it is in dying that we are born to eternal life.

What would you like the Divine Master to grant you?

Lord, make me _____

O Divine Master, grant that I _____

_____

Copy words from the Prayer of St. Francis that especially impress you as being part of Jesus' way of living.

_____   _____

_____   _____

_____   _____

Say the prayer again slowly, substituting your own phrases.

Fourth Sunday in
Ordinary Time

God Reveals Himself to Us through Jesus

Readings: **Deuteronomy 18:15-20; 1 Corinthians 7:32-35; Mark 1:21-28**

Jesus spoke the word of God. He was an expert prophet. Read the following passages:

Deuteronomy 18:18-22   *Mark 1:22-28*

Matthew 7:15-20   *Luke 4:8-19; 7:22-23*

Answer the following:

• How would you describe a prophet? _____

_____

• How can one know if a prophet is true or false? _____

_____

• How did Jesus describe his prophetic ministry? Why was this unusual? _____

_____

• Can you name any modern prophets and tell why you think they are prophets?

1. _____   4. _____

   _____   _____

   _____   _____

2. _____   5. _____

   _____   _____

   _____   _____

3. _____

   _____

   _____

Case Study

Read the following situations. Decide on a prophetic message to give, based on the contents of the Bible and the words and actions of Jesus.

1. Jean has been going steady for almost six months. Her boyfriend says that he thinks they should have sex to see if they are really compatible in love-making. Jean comes to you, her best friend, for advice.

_____

_____

_____

_____

2. Jack feels that he doesn't want to follow in the footsteps of his father and be a farmer. He says there isn't enough money in it. He wants to go to the big city, get a job, have fun, and live it up. He talks to you during the lunch hour.

_____

_____

_____

_____

3. There is going to be a town meeting concerning a projected new chemical plant that is supposed to be built in the area. It will bring in money and jobs, but there are rumors that it may pollute the water. Your father doesn't know too much about this—but you have studied it recently. He asks your advice before going to the meeting that night.

_____

_____

_____

_____

4. There is going to be a party at Joy's house, and her parents are supposed to be away. Jim, your friend, suggests that you both take beer and alcohol from your parents' liquor cupboard so that the party will be a ''good'' one. What do you say to Jim? What about Joy?

_____

_____

_____

_____

5. Bob has his temporary license. His parents leave town one weekend, leaving the second car at home—with the warning that it is not to be used. Bob is invited to a party and really wants to go; however, no one will pick him up because he lives too far out of town. What would you tell him?

_____

_____

_____

_____

6. Betty is supposed to go to religion classes each Wednesday night. She is picked up by Sue. Since Betty doesn't feel she is learning anything, she suggests they go shopping instead. What should Sue say?

_____

_____

_____

_____

Presented to the Lord

Readings: Malachi 3:1-4; Hebrews 2:14-18; Luke 2:22-40

The original name of this feast was Hipopante, or the Meeting of Jesus and Simeon. It was an appropriate title. Jesus meets and is presented to the God of his ancestors in the temple. He meets Simeon and Anna, symbols of all those people who had waited and believed in their God and the Messiah whom God would send.

Israel's story is about a series of meetings between God and His people. These meetings both reveal and veil God's presence. Look up the following passages in the Bible.

Genesis 18:1-15

To whom does God reveal Himself? _____

In what way does God remain hidden? _____

_____

Exodus 33:7-11

To whom does God reveal Himself? _____

In what way does God remain hidden? _____

_____

How is God revealed in the Child whom Mary and Joseph brought to the temple? _____

_____

In what way is God hidden in the Child? _____

_____

Today we recall the meeting of Jesus with Simeon and with Anna. Simeon and Anna symbolized all the people who waited for the coming of the Messiah. Today we use candles to greet Jesus, the true Light who is in our midst. List below three ways we meet Jesus today. Tell how Christ is both revealed and hidden in these meetings.

1. _____
_____
_____
_____

2. _____
_____
_____

3. _____
_____
_____

The feast of Hipopante replaced a pagan Roman celebration which was held on February 2. The Roman celebration was a procession and a purification ceremony. The Church incorporated the procession into the celebration of Hipopante. The gospel story inspired the use of lights in the celebration.

The Church's practice throughout history has often been to welcome the customs and traditions of new Christians. The Church has tried to help these new converts see how the symbols that speak to all human beings are really reflections of God's love. For example, December 25, the day we celebrate as the birthday of the Light of the World, was originally a Roman feast in honor of the sun.

Some Christians object to this practice of adopting pagan feasts and customs into Church celebrations. The Puritans, for example, fined persons for "keeping Christmas." They considered it a way of profaning the gospel. And Spanish Catholics did not always appreciate the positive features of Indian culture and religion.

What do you think? _____
_____
_____
_____

Fifth Sunday in
Ordinary Time

The Lord Loves the Oppressed

Sunday Readings: **Job 7:1-4, 6-7; 1 Corinthians 9:16-19, 22-23; Mark 1:29-39**

The Gospel of Mark shows Jesus reaching out to those in need of healing, in need of being freed from the demons holding them down.

Name some things that hold down you and other people you know, that keep you from acting as free, responsible, and caring human beings. Also tell what kind of effect this has on society.

Cause	Effect
Fear	Prevents people from speaking out for their rights.

_____

_____

_____

_____

Read this account of the life of Saint Martin de Porres.

Martin de Porres (1579–1639)

"Father unknown" is the cold legal phrase for it on baptismal records. "Half-breed" or "war souvenir" is the cruel name inflicted by those of "pure" blood. Like many others, Martin might have grown to be a bitter man, but he did not. It was said that even as a child he gave his heart and his goods to the poor and despised.

He was the illegitimate son of a freed-woman of Panama, probably a Negro but possibly of Indian stock, and a Spanish grandee of Lima, Peru. He inherited the features and dark complexion of his mother, and though this irked his father, he finally acknowledged his son after eight years. After the birth of a sister, he abandoned the family. Martin was reared in poverty, locked into a low level of Lima's society.

At 12 his mother apprenticed him to a barber-surgeon. He learned how to cut hair and also how to draw blood (a standard medical treatment then), care for wounds, and prepare and administer medicines.

After a few years in this medical apostolate, he applied to the Dominicans to be a "lay helper," not feeling himself worthy to be a religious brother. After nine years, the example of his prayer and penance, charity and humility led the community to request him to make full religious profession. Many of his nights were spent in prayer and penitential practices; his days were filled with nursing the sick, caring for the poor. It was particularly impressive that he treated all men regardless of their color, race or status. He was instrumental in founding an orphanage, took care of slaves brought from Africa, and managed the daily alms of the priory with practicality as well as generosity. He became the procurator for both priory and city whether it was a matter of "blankets, shirts, candles, candy, miracles or prayers!" When his priory was in debt, he said, "I am only a poor mulatto. Sell me. I am the property of the Order. Sell me."

Side by side with his daily work in the kitchen, laundry and infirmary, God chose to fill Martin's life with extraordinary gifts: ecstasies that lifted him into the air, light filling the room where he prayed, bilocation, miraculous knowledge, instantaneous cures and a remarkable control over animals. His charity extended to beasts of the field and even to the vermin of the kitchen. He would excuse the raids of mice and rats on the ground that they were underfed, and kept stray cats and dogs at his sister's house.

He became a formidable fund-raiser, obtaining thousands of dollars for dowries for poor girls, so that they could marry or enter a convent.

Many of his fellow religious took him as their spiritual director, but he continued to call himself a "poor slave." He was a good friend of another Dominican saint of Peru, Rose of Lima.

From Saint of the Day, Vol. 2, Leonard Foley (Cincinnati: St. Anthony Messenger Press, 1975), 135-137. Used with permission.

In what ways was Martin de Porres a victim of oppression?

_____

_____

How did he respond?

_____

_____

Describe a person you admire who is acting today to help those who are poor, suffering, or oppressed.

_____

_____

Name one thing you can do to help someone more needy than yourself.

_____

_____

Sixth Sunday in
Ordinary Time

Jesus Cares, We Care

Readings: Leviticus 13:1-2, 44-46; 1 Corinthians 10:31-11:1; Mark 1:40-45

Name a song that speaks of isolation or rejection.

_____

What is the message of the lyrics? _____

_____

What is the cause of the isolation or rejection? _____

_____

_____

How can the isolation or rejection be alleviated? _____

_____

_____

Read the newspaper or listen to area news on the radio or television for stories of persons who are rejected by others or treated as outcasts by society.

Watch what is happening in the halls or in class at school. Who is left out? Who always seems to be alone?

Make a list of at least four persons. Share your observations with your family and with a good friend.

Person(s)	What is happening now	Other possibilities
1. _____	_____	_____
2. _____	_____	_____
3. _____	_____	_____
4. _____		

How can you make a difference?

_____

_____

_____

_____

_____

Society said that lepers had to live apart and keep a distance from all people. But the leper **chose** to move toward Jesus and ask for healing.

Has there been a time in your life when society or friends said you should act in a certain way or when you felt distanced from others, and yet you chose to move toward God and ask God's help?

How did you feel? What happened? Did someone reach out to you? Write your thoughts and feelings about that occasion.

_____

_____

_____

_____

_____

Does your reflection create a deeper meaning for this week's responsorial psalm: "I turn to you, Lord, in time of trouble, and you fill me with the joy of salvation"?

_____

_____

Our Church tradition, past and present, is rich with people who have chosen to live God's life of compassion and love with all people. Listed below are the names of some Christians who have been examples of God's compassion. Choose one of the names. See what information you can find about this person. Share what you have learned with your family.

St. Vincent de Paul   _Archbishop Oscar Romero_

St. Elizabeth of Hungary   _Jean Donovan_

Write a paragraph about someone you know who is a sign of God's compassion.

_____

_____

_____

_____

_____

_____

_____

_____

Prayer

God, I believe that You love me and are always with me.
Help me, God, to reach out and love all people.

Seventh Sunday in
Ordinary Time

Jesus Heals through the Sacraments

Readings: **Isaiah 43:18-19, 21-22, 24-25; 2 Corinthians 1:18-22; Mark 2:1-12**

One very effective way of coming to understand the sacraments and what they do for us is to read the rite of the sacrament. Read the following paragraphs from the introduction to the Rite of the Anointing of the Sick. Then answer the questions below.

> *98. In the course of his visits to the sick, the priest should try to explain two complementary aspects of this sacrament: through the sacrament of anointing the Church supports the sick in their struggle against illness and continues Christ's messianic work of healing. All who are united in the bond of a common baptism and a common faith are joined together in the body of Christ since what happens to one member affects all. The sacrament of anointing effectively expresses the share that each one has in the suffering of others. When the priest anoints the sick, he is anointing in the name and with the power of Christ himself (see Mark 6:13). On behalf of the whole community, he is ministering to those members who are suffering. This message of hope and comfort is also needed by those who care for the sick, especially those who are closely bound in love to them. There should be opportunity for suitable preparation over a period of time for the benefit of the sick themselves and of those who are with them.*
>
> *99. . . . Because of its very nature as a sign, the sacrament of the anointing of the sick should be celebrated with members of the family and other representatives of the Christian community whenever this is possible. Then the sacrament is seen for what it is—a part of the prayer of the Church and an encounter with the Lord.*

What can the Sacrament of Anointing of the Sick do for the one who is anointed?

_____

Who else benefits from the sacrament? _____

Who should be present for the sacrament? Why? _____

There are three distinct aspects of the celebration of the sacrament:

1. "Prayer of faith: The community, asking God's help for the sick, makes its prayer of faith in response to God's word and in a spirit of trust. . . ." (#105)

2. "Laying on of hands. . . . The laying on of hands is clearly a sign of blessing, as we pray that by the power of God's healing grace the sick person may be restored to health or at least strengthened in time of illness. The laying on of hands is also an invocation: the Church prays for the coming of the Holy Spirit upon the sick person. Above all, it is the biblical gesture of healing and indeed Jesus' own usual manner of healing: 'They brought the sick with various diseases to him; and he laid hands on every one of them and healed them' (Luke 4:40)" (#106)

3. "Anointing with oil: The practice of anointing the sick with oil signifies healing, strengthening, and the presence of the Spirit. In the gospel of Mark the disciples were sent out by the Lord to continue his healing ministry: 'They anointed many sick people with oil and cured them' (Mark 6:13). And Saint James witnesses to the fact that the Church continued to anoint the sick with oil as both a means and a sign of healing." (#107)

Read through the Rite for the Anointing of a Sick Person found below. Mark with a * the places in the rite where these three signs occur.

> *The priest greets the sick person and the others present.*
>
> *The peace of the Lord be with you always. R. And also with you.*
>
> *If it seems desirable, the priest may sprinkle the sick person and those present with holy water.*

The Lord is our shepherd / and leads us to streams of living water.

Then he addresses those present in these or similar words:

My dear friends, we are gathered here in the name of our Lord Jesus Christ who is present among us. As the gospels relate, the sick came to him for healing; moreover he loves us so much that he died for our sake. Through the apostle James, he has commanded us: "Are there any sick among you? Let them send for the priests of the Church, and let the priests pray over them anointing them with oil in the name of the Lord; and the prayer of faith will save the sick persons, and the Lord will raise them up; and if they have committed any sins, their sins will be forgiven them." (James 5:14–15) Let us therefore commend our sick brother/sister N. to the grace and power of Christ, that he may save him/her and raise him/her up.

The priest invites the sick person and all present to join in the penitential rite, which follows one of the forms used in the Mass. Then one of those present or the priest reads a brief text from scripture. This is followed by a brief period of silence and/or a brief explanation of the reading applying it to the sick person and those who are caring for him/her.

The priest may adapt or shorten the following litany according to the condition of the sick person.

My brothers and sisters, in our prayer of faith let us appeal to God for our brother/sister N.

Come and strengthen him/her through this holy anointing: Lord have mercy.
R. Lord have mercy.

Free him/her from all harm. R.

Free him/her from sin and all temptation. R.

Relieve the sufferings of all the sick. R.

Assist all those dedicated to the care of the sick. R.

Give life and health to our brother/sister N., on whom we lay our hands in your name. R.

In silence, the priest lays his hands on the head of the sick person.

If the oil is already blessed, the priest says a prayer of thanksgiving over blessed oil. (The oil was blessed by the bishop on Holy Thursday. Sometimes the priest will bless the oil at this time.)

Praise to you, God, the almighty Father. / You sent your Son to live among us / and bring us salvation.
R. Blessed be God who heals us in Christ.

Praise to you, God, the only-begotten Son. / You humbled yourself to share in our humanity / and you heal our infirmities. R.

Praise to you, God, the Holy Spirit, the Consoler, / Your unfailing power gives us strength in our bodily weakness. R.

God of mercy, ease the sufferings and comfort the weakness / of your servant N., whom the Church anoints with this holy oil. / We ask this through Christ our Lord.
R. Amen.

The priest anoints the sick person with the blessed oil. First he anoints the forehead, saying:

Through this holy anointing / may the Lord in his love and mercy help you / with the grace of the Holy Spirit.
R. Amen.

Then he anoints the hands saying:

May the Lord who frees you from sin / save you and raise you up.
R. Amen. . . .

Let us pray.
Father in heaven, / through this holy anointing / grant N. comfort in his(her) suffering.
When he(she) is afraid, give him(her) courage, / when afflicted, give him(her) patience, / when dejected, afford him(her) hope, / and when alone, assure him(her) of the support of your holy people.
We ask this through Christ our Lord. R. Amen.

The rite concludes with the Lord's Prayer and the priest's blessing.

Eighth Sunday in
Ordinary Time

Friendship

Readings: **Hosea 2:16-17, 21-22; 2 Corinthians 3:1-6; Mark 2:18-22**

Dating is a part of growing and learning about ourselves and persons of the other sex. Use the following chart to reflect on the meaning of dating in your life.

Jesus	Me
Concerned with the inner self as well as customs and rules	Do I get caught up with the expectations of peers?
People and how they treat one another is the guideline	Who or what forms my opinions or serves as my guide for dating?
Like new wineskins; open to growth and change	Do I anticipate a certain response? Have I become hardened by past experiences? Is our relationship growing? Do we spend time with other people?
Concerned with the inner qualities of persons	What is most important to me in choosing a date?

Complete the following chart using numbers from 0 (not present) to 5 (excellent) in each category

	Me	Best Friend	Date
Kind			
Slow to anger			
Faithful			
Forgiving			
Generous			
Understanding			

The qualities listed above describe God's relationship (covenant) of love with each of us. Husbands and wives are to be signs in and to the world of Christ's love for his people.

We learn a great deal about love and marriage from TV, music, and movies. But often the view of marriage presented is contrary to Christ's message. Find examples from the following media which go directly against Christ's teaching about love and marriage.

movies _____

_____

TV programs _____

_____

songs _____

_____

Christian marriage is a sign of God's love for His people. Such love is unconditional. Within marriage, sexual intercourse is the symbol of the love between the husband and the wife. It is both a deep sharing of unconditional love between the partners and a source of the possibility of new life. Such total love is found only in and is supported by the Sacrament of Marriage, where the love may continue to grow. Because they value marriage so much, Christians believe that genital sexual activity outside of marriage is wrong. Any acts that lead directly to sexual intercourse are also reserved for those who are committed to one another in marriage.

Are there any TV shows, movies, or songs that support the Christian view of love and marriage? Give one example and tell how it supports Christ's ideal.

_____

_____

The young person who strives to live up to Christ's standards is in for a difficult struggle. As Christians, we are called to be different. We are called to witness to the beauty and holiness of human sexuality and its rootedness in the total commitment of marriage. The discipline required to live by Christ's standards can prepare us well for marriage. We can find support for our struggle in our relationship with Jesus Christ. Personal prayer and frequent use of the sacraments is a source of strength for us.

Make a list of attitudes and actions which can be helpful in building the kind of healthy relationships which will lead to a good marriage.

_____

_____

_____

_____

Make a list of attitudes and actions which might threaten future relationships in marriage.

_____

_____

_____

_____

The gospel speaks of fasting. How familiar are you with fasting? The experience of giving something up or doing without "empties a person." It may create a hunger for what you have chosen to give up. Can you really understand thirst if you have never been thirsty? Can you really understand hunger if you've never been hungry? Fasting challenges us to examine whether we really have control of our lives or whether we let food, TV, or other outside influences control us. Creating an "empty space" can be a healthy way to make room for God. When we make more room for God, fasting is helping us to build our relationship with God. We can call on God for help when we are tempted to break our fast.

Choose something that is a favorite part of your life—a food, TV, the presence of music whenever you're in the car or doing homework, pop, etc. Fast from whatever you have chosen for this week. Use the space below as your journal for daily reflections as you "create an emptiness."

_____

_____

_____

_____

_____

Sundays Are Special

Readings: **Deuteronomy 5:12–15; 2 Corinthians 4:6–11; Mark 2:23–3:6**

Memories of your growing up will be with you forever. Right now you have memories of favorite times with your family. What are some of the memories you have of your family and the way they spend their Sundays?

Remembering also plays an important part in Catholic Sunday worship. The Church assembles each Sunday at Eucharist to recall the saving acts of the Lord Jesus, to hear God's word, to offer bread and wine, and to share in Jesus' sacramental body and blood.

How long has the Church been doing this? (For a clue, read **1 Corinthians 11:23–34.**)

_____

_____

Why does the Church come together to offer bread and wine and to share the body and blood of Christ? **(1 Corinthians 11:23–25**

_____

_____

Participation in Sunday worship is so important to the Church that it heads the list of seven duties expected of Catholic Christians.

Why do you think the Sunday Eucharist is so important to the Church?

_____

_____

How could celebrating Sunday Eucharist help a person live more faithfully as a Christian? _____

_____

What purpose is fulfilled by community worship that cannot be fulfilled by praying alone? _____

_____

31

Jesus grew up in a family which observed Sabbath, the Jewish weekly holy day. *Sabbath,* which means "rest" or "cease," involves keeping the day holy and resting from labor. To understand how serious the obligation to cease from labor was among some Jews, read the story told in the book of **Numbers 15: 32-36.**

Scripture tells us that Jesus observed the Sabbath. He sometimes taught in the synagogue on the Sabbath. In light of your understanding of how important Sabbath observance was to the Jews and of Jesus' respect for the Sabbath, read **Mark 2:23-3:6.**

Name the ways Jesus violates the Sabbath, according to his critics.

_____

_____

What single sentence sums up Jesus' position on Sabbath observance? _____

_____

For the Jewish people, celebrating the Sabbath was and is a way of consecrating all of time to God. It is a way of acknowledging that God is Lord of all creation. The world is not our possession. Everything we have is a gift. Human beings are often tempted to forget this truth. We use the land, trees, water, minerals, plants and animals, and even the air as our own absolute possession. Sometimes we want to control all of life.

The Sabbath is a day to recognize that God has given us creation as a gift. Recognizing this gift from our loving Creator, we relax our control and enjoy the good things God has created. The Sabbath is a day to renew our friendship with God and to increase our appreciation for the good things God has given us, for our families and friends.

Jesus said that the Sabbath was made for people and not the other way around. What can observance of the Lord's day do for people?

_____

_____

_____

What are some ways that you cease from labor on Sundays and keep it holy? _____

_____

_____

A New Beginning

Readings: **Genesis 9:8-15; 1 Peter 3:18-22; Mark 1:12-15**

Lent is a period of preparation for the celebration of Easter, the most important celebration of the Church year. Originally, Lent was a period of fasting for the catechumens who would be baptized at the Easter celebration. At first this time of fasting lasted only a few days. Gradually the time was lengthened to forty days to correspond to the forty days Jesus fasted in the desert.

Lent also became a time for people who had fallen away from the Church to return. During Lent they would do penance. They would be reconciled with the Church on Holy Thursday so that they could join the community in the celebration of the paschal mystery.

Today, as in the ancient Church, Lent is a time for catechumens to prepare for baptism at the Easter Vigil. It is also a time for baptized Christians to prepare to renew their baptism. It is a time to make a new beginning.

The decision to follow Jesus is never a commitment we make once and for all. There are always temptations to follow our own desires and to put our relationship with Jesus in second place. Lent is a time to refocus our lives on God. Three Lenten practices which help us to refocus our lives are prayer, fasting, and almsgiving.

Fasting

Fasting of some kind is practiced in many religions. Some people fast by taking only liquid nourishment. Some people fast by eating nothing from sunrise to sunset. Catholics today fast on Ash Wednesday and Good Friday by eating only one full meal and two smaller meals and nothing in between meals. Only Catholics between the ages of twenty-one and fifty-nine are required by Church law to keep the fast. But Catholics at any age can fast from something such as eating between meals or watching TV. The important thing about fasting is that it helps us focus our lives on God.

What kind of fasting do you think would help you to focus your life on God?

_____

_____

_____

_____

_____

_____

Prayer

Lent is a time to renew our friendship with God. This is a time when Christians spend extra time in reading the Bible, praying the rosary, or making the way of the cross. It may be the time to begin a practice of meditation or a time to take a quiet walk with God in the woods.

What kind of prayer do you think would help you renew your friendship with God?

_____

_____

_____

_____

_____

_____

Almsgiving

An essential part of being a Christian is caring for one another. This is a time when Christians think of the poor and the suffering. We use the money we would use for our own entertainment or pleasure to give to the poor instead. Sometimes we prepare simple, inexpensive meals during Lent in order to be able to help the poor. But we can also find other ways of caring for one another. We can visit someone who is sick or do some task for someone who is unable to do it for themselves.

What practices of almsgiving will help you to refocus your life on God?

_____

_____

_____

_____

_____

_____

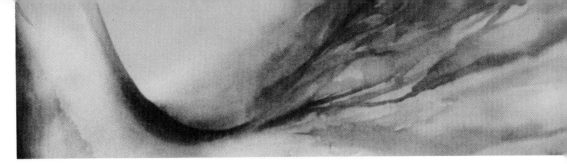

Second Sunday of
Lent

The Cost of Discipleship

Readings: **Genesis 22:1-2, 9, 10-13, 15-18; Romans 8:31-34; Mark 9:2-10**

St. Ignatius outlined a method of meditation which he taught to people. Meditation is a method of prayer which helps us to grow closer to God. Use this method as you think and pray about the story of the Transfiguration.

1. Set a mood for prayer. Find a quiet place and sit quietly for a few minutes. You may wish to light a candle or turn down the lights. Slowly read the gospel story for today: **Mark 9:2-10.**

2. Imagine yourself climbing the mountain with Jesus and Peter, James, and John. What do you see? What do you feel? What do you taste? Hear?

3. Imagine you see Jesus transfigured before you. Imagine the radiance of Jesus' body, the feeling of joy and peace. What do you hear God saying to you?

4. You are walking back down the mountain with Jesus. How do you feel? What do you want to say?

5. Talk to Jesus. Tell him about your hopes and fears. Ask him for the help you need to live as a Christian.

Imagine that you are the apostle Peter. Like the other apostles, you have been preaching the good news of Jesus' death and resurrection. The authorities have been trying to get you to stop, and they have put you in prison. This is not the first time you have been in prison for preaching about Jesus. You know that many Christians are finding it hard to live their faith in these trying times. You remember your experience of the transfiguration of Jesus and how that experience helped you to believe in Jesus. You write to the Christian community to encourage them. Write your letter here.

Dear Friends,

_____

_____

_____

_____

_____

_____

_____

_____

_____

_____

_____

_____

_____

_____

When you have finished, read **2 Peter 1:12–19.** This letter was probably written between A.D. 100 and 115. Although the letter claims to be written by Peter (who died between A.D. 64 and 67), it was probably written by another Christian leader—in the spirit of Peter's thought—to encourage Christians during a time of persecution.

The Covenant

Readings: **Exodus 20:1-17; 1 Corinthians 1:22-25, John 2:13-25**

In the fall of 1987, newspapers in the Midwest carried a story reporting the trial of a group of teenagers in a small southern Missouri town. The teenagers had been involved in a form of Satan worship. One of the requirements for belonging to the group was human sacrifice. A group of teenagers bludgeoned to death a local teenager who was an outcast among his peers.

In the spring of 1989, the newspaper of a small Kansas town reported on the activities of Satanists in that town. The cult was related to the local drug traffic, it was said. Citizens speculated on the relationship between the cult and several local murders the town officials had been unable to solve. High school students reported being pressured to attend meetings of Satanic groups.

Why do you think people get involved with Satanic cults? _____

_____

Satanic worship is a direct challenge to Christian faith. While Christian faith places God at the center of one's life, Satanism sets out to deny God that place. Satanic ceremonies involve desecration of what Christians hold sacred. Sometimes these are religious objects, even the Blessed Sacrament. Often it involves deliberate attempts to pervert our natural human compassion. Human beings have a natural tendency to want to treat animals and other people kindly. Cruelty to animals and to human beings, even murder, are included in Satanic ceremonies. Sexual perversion, an affront to the human person as the dwelling place of the Spirit, may also be included in the cult.

One observer has suggested that Satanic worship grows when organized religion becomes weak. Do you think this is true? Why or why not?

_____

_____

Mark with an S those elements which can be found in Satanism. Mark with a C those elements which can be found in the Church.

____ *Belonging*   ____ *Mystery*   ____ *Ritual*   ____ *Confusion*

____ *Power*   ____ *Love*   ____ *Honesty*

The readings chosen for the third Sunday of Lent all emphasize the importance of having God as the central focus of our lives. The first reading is the Ten Commandments, the law which was to govern the lives of faithful Israelites. In the gospel, Jesus chases the merchants out of the temple because they have turned God's house into a marketplace. The second reading points out that we often do not understand God's ways. God's ways may at times seem foolish to us, but God's foolishness is wiser than our wisdom.

Most of us aren't tempted a great deal by Satanism or even by other less serious occult practices. But we do find ourselves facing the temptation to put something else besides God at the center of our lives. We find ourselves rationalizing to make something we know is wrong seem perfectly all right. Sometimes the temptation comes through friends. Often it comes from the culture around us, which convinces us that our lives should be focused on something else—like making money or being popular. The culture, our friends, and even our own rationalizing can make God's ways seem foolish.

From the earliest days of the Church, prayers of exorcism have been part of the preparation for baptism. The Church prays that the lives of the catechumens, now called the *elect,* may be changed by the word of God so that they may overcome their weakness through God's power. On the third, fourth, and fifth Sundays of Lent, the Church prays that the elect may be freed from the power of evil so that they may live as children of God. At the Easter Vigil, the elect and the whole community promise to reject Satan and his works.

Two forms may be used at the Easter Vigil:

Option 1

Priest: *Do you reject Satan?*
All: *I do.*
Priest: *And all his works?*
All: *I do.*
Priest: *And all his empty promises?*
All: *I do.*

Option 2

Priest: *Do you reject sin, so as to live in the freedom of God's children?*
All: *I do.*
Priest: *Do you reject the glamour of evil and refuse to be mastered by sin?*
All: *I do.*
Priest: *Do you reject Satan, father of sin and prince of darkness?*
All: *I do.*

Which of these forms do you find more meaningful? _____

One of the ways of seeking forgiveness of sin today is the reconciliation service that will be held in your parish church during Lent. As preparation for participation in this communal celebration, let us review what happens when you talk with Father.

Welcome: *The priest will welcome you in the name of Jesus and the Church (the People of God). With the priest, you will make the sign of the cross. "In the name. . . ."*

God's Word (with all earlier or individual here): *You will hear God's Word in the penance celebration. The priest will recall with you the goodness, kindness, and forgiveness of our loving God, who heals us of our selfishness and strengthens us to do God's will.*

Forgiveness and Healing: *We ask God to hear our confession of sin and of praise for His forgiveness. We ask God to change us, forgive us, heal us . . . .*

God, I ask You to heal me of . . . .
Lord, I need a change of this attitude . . . .
Lord Jesus, help me to overcome my habit of . . . .

Penance: *The priest will ask you to pray and/or do some act of service to help you grow in following Jesus and his way.*

Prayer of Sorrow: *You may pray an Act of Contrition (Sorrow) you know or choose one of these:*

God, my loving Father, I am sorry for my sins. I ask Your forgiveness and healing. I will work at being more like Your Son Jesus. Please send me Your Spirit to help me love You and my neighbor. Amen.

Jesus, you came to proclaim forgiveness. Forgive my sins. Send your Spirit into my life to make me less selfish and more attuned to living your Way in my life. Amen.

Laying on of Hands and Absolution: *The priest lays his hands on your head as a sign of God's love, forgiveness, and healing. He says:*

God, the Father of mercies,
through the death and resurrection of His Son,
has reconciled the world to Himself
and sent the Holy Spirit among us
for the forgiveness of sins,
through the ministry of the Church.

May God give you pardon and peace,
and I absolve you from your sins
in the name of the Father,
and of the Son,
and of the Holy Spirit.
(The priest will make the Sign of the Cross over you.)
Answer: *Amen.*

Priest: *The Lord has freed you from your sins and healed you.*
Answer: *Thank you, Father.*

Grace

Readings: 2 Chronicles 36:14-17, 19-23; Ephesians 2:4-10; John 3:14-21

Jesus said to Nicodemus, "Just as Moses lifted up the serpent in the desert, so must the Son of Man be lifted up, that all who believe may have eternal life in him." (John 3:14-15)

Moses was leading the Israelite people out of slavery in Egypt. On their way to the Promised Land, they had to pass through the desert. The journey was long and hard. The Bible says it took them forty years.

The Book of Numbers 21:4-9 tells the story of Moses lifting up the serpent.

The Bronze Serpent

From Mount Hor they set out on the Red Sea road to bypass the land of Edom. But with their patience worn out by the journey, the people complained against God and Moses, "Why have you brought us up from Egypt to die in this desert, where there is no food or water? We are disgusted with this wretched food!"

In punishment the Lord sent among the people saraph serpents, which bit the people so that many of them died. Then the people came to Moses and said, "We have sinned in complaining against the Lord and you. Pray the Lord to take the serpents from us." So Moses prayed for the people, and the Lord said to Moses, "Make a saraph and mount it on a pole, and if anyone who has been bitten looks at it, he will recover." Moses accordingly made a bronze serpent and mounted it on a pole, and whenever anyone who had been bitten by a serpent looked at the bronze serpent, he recovered.

Why did Moses raise up the bronze serpent?

_____

Who was saved when Moses lifted up the serpent?

_____

In what way is Jesus like the bronze serpent?

_____

_____

_____

_____

Who is saved because Jesus was lifted up on the cross?

_____

_____

_____

_____

_____

_____

The caduceus is used as a symbol for a pharmacist or a physician. The venom of some snakes is used to make the antidote which is used to heal persons bitten by the same snakes.

Think about how much God loves us. Does God love us when we complain? _____

_____

Recall five complaints you have had in the last few days.

_____

_____

_____

_____

_____

Write five good things (blessings) that happened.

_____

_____

_____

_____

_____

Did some of your complaints get changed to blessings? _____

Read Psalm 23 slowly. God's loving care for His servant David is shown by the shepherd's care for his sheep (1-4) and a host's generosity toward a guest.

The Lord is my shepherd; I shall not want.
   In verdant pastures he gives me repose;
Beside restful waters he leads me;
   he refreshes my soul.
He guides me in right paths
   for his name's sake.
Even though I walk in the dark valley,
   I fear no evil; for you are at my side.

With your rod and your staff
   that give me courage.
You spread the table before me
   in the sight of my foes;
You anoint my head with oil;
   my cup overflows.
Only goodness and kindness follow me
   all the days of my life.
And I shall dwell in the house of the Lord
   for years to come.

Fifth Sunday of Lent

Paschal Mystery

Readings: Jeremiah 31:31–34; Hebrews 5:7–9; John 12:20–33

> *. . . unless the grain of wheat falls to the earth and dies, it remains just a grain of wheat.*
> *But if it dies, it produces much fruit. (John 12:24)*

The cycle of death and life which Jesus describes in this passage is a truth that is emphasized in many religions. The ancient Egyptians told a myth about the phoenix, a bird something like an eagle. Every five hundred years, so the myth goes, the bird burned itself to death. This made possible the birth of a new phoenix out of the ashes of the old one. The meaning of the myth for the Egyptians was that the dust and ashes that result from death are the materials out of which new life can come.

This cycle is also visible in nature. New life grows, fertilized by the decomposition of last year's growth. Night gives way to morning. The butterfly emerges as a new creation from the caterpillar's cocoon. Seeds must "die" in order to go on living. Even the cells in our bodies are constantly being replaced by new ones.

Name two other examples of life emerging from death that you can see in nature.

1. _____

2. _____

The same mystery of life which emerges from death can be seen in our own inner lives. The infant must give up the security of the womb in order to live. A teenager gives up the securities of childhood in order to take on responsibility as a maturing person. The person who wants to be a musician or an athlete must give up something in order to gain this new identity.

Give two examples of "deaths" you have endured in order to gain new life.

1. _____

2. _____

Failure, rejection, suffering, and physical death are "deaths" we all fear. No one wants to be a failure, and experiencing even small failures can be very painful. We fear both physical pain and the emotional pain of rejection. And, even though we may not think about it much, we also fear our own death. Yet that, too, will happen. In times of great tragedy or natural disaster, we wonder, "What can this mean?"

Jesus also experienced this kind of "death." Look up the following passages. Match the Scripture reference in Column A with one of the "deaths" in Column B.

Column A

____ Matthew 11:20–24

____ John 6:53–66

____ Luke 4:14–30

____ Matthew 26:38–39

____ John 11: 33–35

Column B

a. rejection

b. death

c. failure

d. suffering

Think about a time when you experienced one of these *deaths*. Did new life come from this "death"?

_____

_____

_____

_____

On the cross Jesus faced and overcame death in all its forms. His death on the cross and his resurrection on the third day reveal most clearly the mystery of God's plan for the world. We call it the *Paschal Mystery.*

Jesus accepted the death that came to him because he continued to do God's will. He reversed the choice made by the first human beings. They chose to do their own will, and the results of that choice were sin, suffering, and death. Jesus gave the human race a new beginning. He chose to do the will of God, even though he knew it would mean his own death. He did not retaliate with violence against his enemies, and he continued to do and say what he knew God wanted him to do and say, even though he knew it would lead to his death. In his death, Jesus showed that the Father was the absolute center of his life. He showed the depth of God's love for us. Because he chose to do the will of God, Jesus became the source of eternal life for his followers. By his death, Jesus brought life to the whole world.

Holy Week

Readings: **Mark 11:1-10; Isaiah 50:4-7; Philippians 2:6-11; Mark 14:1-15:47**

This Thursday evening we begin the Easter Triduum, the great Three Days. The Triduum is the high point and central celebration of the entire liturgical year. Lent ends on Thursday, and the Triduum begins with the evening Mass of the Lord's Supper. On Good Friday and, if possible, on Holy Saturday, we observe the Easter fast. It is a time to fast from food and work and entertainment. This is not a sad or penitential fast. It is an eager anticipation for the Easter Vigil when the elect will be baptized and we will renew our own baptism. It is a time for both personal prayer and community prayer. At various times during these three days, the community of faith gathers to worship.

In what ways does fasting from food, work, and entertainment help us to enter more fully into the paschal mystery?

_____

_____

_____

Holy Thursday

On Holy Thursday the community gathers to celebrate the Lord's Supper. This was the night that Jesus gave himself to us in the Holy Eucharist. It was also the night before he died. Jesus washed the feet of his disciples and gave us an example of how we ought to love and serve others. And it's the night the Church celebrates the institution of Holy Orders. At the end of the service, the Eucharistic bread and wine are reserved for communion on Good Friday.

Spend some time tonight watching and praying with Jesus. **Read John 14 to 17** slowly and prayerfully. What is Jesus saying to you?

_____

_____

_____

_____

_____

_____

Good Friday

On Friday we fast from whatever would distract us from the great mystery we celebrate (television might be an example). Like children too excited to eat, we look forward to the Easter celebration. On Friday afternoon or Friday evening, the community gathers to read the story of Jesus' suffering and death. We pray for the needs of the whole Church. We venerate the cross, sign of Christ's victory over death. We receive Holy Communion and enter into the mystery of Jesus' self-giving.

Many customs have arisen around the observance of Good Friday. Some Christians meet for worship from noon to 3:00 p.m. to remember the time that Jesus hung on the cross. Others observe a time of quiet prayer in their homes during this time. Some use this time to plant a spring garden, burying the seeds that will soon rise to new life.

Is there a custom your family observes on Good Friday? What is it? How does it help you to enter into the paschal mystery?

_____

_____

How do other families you know observe this day?

_____

_____

Holy Saturday

This is a day to continue watching and praying. It is also a day to anticipate the joy of Easter.

Tonight the community gathers to begin the celebration of the resurrection in the Easter Vigil. It is a day to baptize new Catholic Christians and to renew our own baptism.

Although there are nine readings assigned for the vigil, most parishes choose to read only four or five of the readings. Unless we have read all of the readings beforehand, however, we may miss the story the readings tell. Take some time today to read these readings which summarize the meaning of our life as Christians.

1. Genesis 1:1–2:2
2. Genesis 22:1–18
3. Exodus 14:15–15:1
4. Isaiah 54:5–14
5. Isaiah 55:1–11

6. Baruch 3:9–15, 32–4:4
7. Ezekiel 36:16–28
   Epistle: Romans 6:3–11
   Gospel: Mark 16:1–18

Underline the readings that are used at your parish celebration of the Easter Vigil this year.

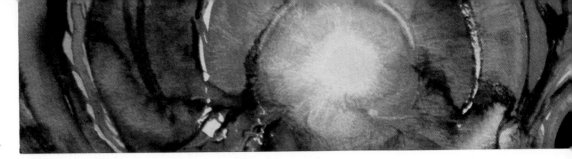

Easter Sunday

The Lord Is Risen

Readings: Acts 10:34, 37–43; Colossians 3:1–4 or 1 Corinthians 5:6–8; John 20:1–9 or Mark 16:1–8

The Easter Vigil opens with a light service. We bless the fire. We bless the Paschal candle which will burn in the sanctuary whenever the community gathers for Eucharist during the Easter season. We light other candles from this symbol of Christ our light. In a darkened church lit only by our candles, we listen to the Easter proclamation, also called the *Exultet*. In poetic language the deacon proclaims the meaning of this feast.

Imagine that you want to help your youth group enter into the spirit of the Exultet. In order to do this, you decide to use your camera to take slides of local scenes which illustrate the meaning of Easter for you. Beside each verse of the Exultet below, write what slide you would use to illustrate it. Tell why you think this is a good choice.

—————————————————
—————————————————
—————————————————

Rejoice, heavenly powers! Sing choirs of angels!
Exult, all creation around God's throne!
Jesus Christ, our King, is risen!
Sound the trumpet of salvation!

—————————————————
—————————————————
—————————————————

Rejoice, O earth, in shining splendor,
radiant in the brightness of your King!
Christ has conquered! Glory fills you!
Darkness vanishes for ever!

—————————————————
—————————————————
—————————————————

Rejoice, O Mother Church! Exult in glory!
The risen Savior shines upon you!
Let this place resound with joy,
echoing the mighty song of all God's people!

—————————————————
—————————————————
—————————————————

It is truly right
that with full hearts and minds and voices
we should praise the unseen God, the all-powerful Father,
and his only Son, our Lord Jesus Christ.

—————————————————
—————————————————

For Christ has ransomed us with his blood,
and paid for us the price of Adam's sin
to our eternal Father!

—————————————————
—————————————————

This is our passover feast,
when Christ, the true Lamb, is slain,
whose blood consecrates the homes of all believers.

—————————————————
—————————————————

This is the night when first you saved our fathers:
you freed the people of Israel from their slavery
and led them dry-shod through the sea.

—————————————————

This is the night when the pillar of fire
destroyed the darkness of sin!

_____ This is the night when Christians everywhere,
_____ washed clean of sin
_____ and freed from all defilement,
_____ are restored to grace and grow together in holiness.

_____ This is the night when Jesus Christ
_____ broke the chains of death
_____ and rose triumphant from the grave.

_____ What good would life have been to us,
_____ had Christ not come as our Redeemer?

_____ Father, how wonderful your care for us!
_____ How boundless your merciful love!
_____ To ransom a slave
_____ you gave away your Son.

_____ O happy fault, O necessary sin of Adam,
_____ which gained for us so great a Redeemer!

_____ Most blessed of all nights, chosen by God
_____ to see Christ rising from the dead!

_____ Of this night scripture says:
_____ "The night will be as clear as day:
_____ it will become my light, my joy."

_____ The power of this holy night
_____ dispels all evil, washes guilt away,
_____ restores lost innocence, brings mourners joy;
_____ it casts out hatred, brings us peace, and humbles earthly pride.

_____ Night truly blessed when heaven is wedded to earth
_____ and we are reconciled with God!

_____ Therefore, heavenly Father, in the joy of this night,
_____ receive our evening sacrifice of praise,
_____ your Church's solemn offering.

_____ Accept this Easter candle,
_____ a flame divided but undimmed,
_____ a pillar of fire that glows to the honor of God.

_____ Let it mingle with the lights of heaven
_____ and continue bravely burning
_____ to dispel the darkness of this night!

_____ May the Morning Star which never sets find this flame still
burning;
_____ Christ, that Morning Star, who came back from the dead,
_____ and shed his peaceful light on all mankind,
your Son who lives and reigns for ever and ever. Amen.

Witnesses to the Resurrection

Readings: Acts 4:32-35; 1 John 5:1-6; John 20:19-31

Can you think of something that happened in your life that was a tragedy or seemed like a tragedy at the time? How did you feel? How did you deal with your feelings? Did it change your life? What do you think and feel about it now?

_____

_____

_____

_____

_____

_____

_____

_____

_____

The apostles were shaken up by the death of Jesus. They had had such hopes for Jesus and for themselves as his friends. Like campaign workers after their candidate has lost an election, the apostles were mourning the loss of their dreams as well as the death of their friend Jesus. They gathered to help each other figure out what it all meant. As they gathered, an amazing thing happened. **Read John 20:19-31.**

Why do you think Jesus appeared? _____

_____

What did he do? _____

What did he tell them to do? _____

Their faith in Jesus helped them believe in what he said. It changed their attitude from fear to courage.

Think of the event you wrote about above. What helped you get through those times?

_____

_____

Who were the people who helped you the most? _____

_____

The Paschal Mystery

Christian faith is Easter faith. We believe that Jesus Christ has conquered sin and death through his death and resurrection. In his sufferings, Jesus experienced the forces of evil, sin, and death. But Jesus overcame them in the power of the resurrection.

Because he has risen, Jesus also shares with us the power of his resurrection. Because of this power, we too can overcome evil, sin, and death in our lives and in our world. We also believe that death will not be the end of our lives. We look forward to a new life. We do not know what our new life will be like, but we believe that our lives will be changed rather than ended.

Imagine that a friend comes to you and tells you of a difficulty in his or her life. What could you tell your friend that would be helpful during this time?

_____

_____

_____

_____

_____

Prayer is a way of life which allows you to find a stillness in the midst of the world where you open your hands to God's promises and find hope for yourself, your friends, and the whole community. (Henri Nouwen)

Write about a time when prayer has helped you find hope.

_____

_____

_____

_____

48

We Live a New Life

Readings: Acts 3:13-15, 17-19; 1 John 2:1-5; Luke 24:35-48

Read the situations below. Tell how the attitudes of the persons compare to the teaching of Jesus.

"I don't get mad, I get even." reads the bumper sticker on the back of a truck in the parking lot.

_____

_____

Tracy's sister was killed in an automobile accident. The driver of the car had been drinking. He is facing charges of manslaughter. "I hope he goes to prison," says Tracy. "He should pay for what he did to my sister."

_____

_____

Sixteen-year-old Hugh McEvoy is dead, shot by a thirteen-year-old gunman. The young gunman and his accomplice showed no remorse for the shooting. Hugh's father, a state parole officer said, "I hope the boys have an opportunity to rehabilitate themselves. My son would want me to forgive them."

_____

_____

_____

If you feel inclined to strike back at someone who has hurt you, you are not bad, you are normal. But Jesus offers us a new way of life. He tells us to love our enemies and pray for our persecutors. He teaches us to forgive as God forgives. On the cross, Jesus prayed for his tormentors. "Father, forgive them," he prayed, "for they know not what they do."

Think about your own personal experiences with forgiveness, both receiving forgiveness and offering forgiveness. What happened that needed forgiving? How did the forgiveness come about? How did you feel before the forgiveness? How did you feel afterward? Write about it here.

_____

_____

_____

_____

_____

_____

49

In her little book, *Learning to Forgive*, Doris Donnelly describes what happens to people when they do not forgive. She tells the story of a wealthy mother who cut her daughter out of her will.

> *The exclusion from the will wasn't a surprise to the daughter, at least, not totally. Ten years before the mother's death, in the middle of an acerbic and protracted family argument, the daughter commiserated with her two aunts, the mother's sisters, who represented the opposite point of view in the family feud.*
>
> *The details of the arguments and the merits of each side are not very important, and so will be omitted here. Let it be said, simply, that both mother and daughter perceived the issues and solutions differently, but while the daughter was able to live within the tension of disagreement with her mother, the mother interpreted the daughter's independent vote as "defiance" and "betrayal." Deeply angered, the mother regarded the daughter's behavior as something she was unable to forgive, and she vowed that someday the daughter would pay for "taking sides" against her.*
>
> *To effect the punishment, the mother wasted no time in alerting other members of the family to her displeasure at the daughter's injudicious action. She burned the daughter's pictures, refused her telephone calls, and returned her letters unopened. In hurt and anger, she continued to widen the gulf between them—a chasm that the daughter and other family members tried unsuccessfully to bridge. The final gesture, executed with elaborate attention to legal detail, involved excluding the daughter from the will.*
>
> *For the mother, there was no alternative, no compromising the retaliation she had devoted herself to with such determination and passion. The thought that was particularly loathsome to the mother was bequeathing a life of comfort and luxury to someone who had inflicted on her such embarrassment and pain. Presumably an inheritance through the will would have accomplished just that and had to be avoided at any cost.*
>
> *Some might judge that cost to be excessive, since the mother spent the last ten years of her life, until she died at sixty-eight, vigorously campaigning against a reconciliation. There are those who say that, at the end, she was more adamantly resolved than ever not to forgive, so that she could wreak her final stroke of retaliation from her grave.*
>
> *What happens when people don't forgive? Several things, all of them unpleasant and unhealthy.*

The story above suggests ten probabilities.

1. They are led by their anger, pain, or hatred.

2. They are directed by negative memories.

3. They do not act freely.

4. They keep a controlling grasp on situations and people.

5. They are pressured by lives of tension and stress.

6. They probably shorten their lives.

7. Their relationships with others are strained.

8. Their relationship with God is weakened.

9. They live with feelings of little self-worth.

10. They feel unrelieved guilt.

Reprinted with permission of Macmillan Publishing Company from Learning to Forgive by Doris Donnelly. Copyright © 1979 by Doris Donnelly.

Think about your own experiences of forgiving and not forgiving. Reread the probabilities which Doris Donnelly suggests. Choose one of them and tell why you think it is true.

_____

_____

_____

Tell how the life of the wealthy woman and her daughter would have been different if the woman had lived Jesus' new life of forgiveness.

_____

_____

_____

Fourth Sunday of
Easter

Following Jesus

Readings: Acts 4:8-12; 1 John 3:1-2; John 10:11-18

The Good Shepherd

The imagery of sheep and shepherds is used often in the Bible. Studying some of those passages can help us better understand today's gospel reading.

Look up the following passages to find the answers to the questions below.

Ezekiel 34:1-16 What had the unworthy shepherds done? _____
_____

What did God promise His sheep? _____
_____

Are there situations today where those in authority mistreat those they should serve? Give one example.
_____
_____

Ezekiel 34:17-24 How had the sheep treated one another? _____
_____

What current situations can you think of which this passage could describe? _____
_____

What does God promise His sheep? _____
_____

Isaiah 40:9-11 How will God treat His people? _____
_____

John 10:11-18 Jesus says he is the **Good** Shepherd. How is he different from the poor shepherds?
_____
_____

Who were some of the "other sheep" to whom Jesus reached out? How did people react to the "other sheep" Jesus invited in? _____

_____

_____

Are there people today whom **we** tend to exclude from our "flock?" Who? Why?

_____

_____

_____

_____

One person remarked that our pictures of the Good Shepherd usually show a bright clean Jesus in a meadow with fluffy white sheep around. But that is not a very good picture of real sheep and real shepherds. Taking care of the sheep means taking care of the weak as well as the strong, the sick and the healthy, the even tempered and the nasty ones. Jesus reached out to the tax collectors and the poor, the prostitutes, and other outcasts. He invited them all into his flock.

What are some ways the Church is trying to reach out to the "other sheep"?

_____

_____

_____

_____

_____

_____

Vine and Branches

Readings: Acts 9:26–31; 1 John 3:18–24; John 15:1–8

At a meeting of physicians, the doctors discussed how they felt when one of their patients died. Despite all they had done to try to save the patient, most of them said they felt extremely guilty—as though they were responsible for the person's death. Many of them also said that it so difficult to cope with their feelings in this regard that they deliberately tried to shield themselves from feeling anything at all. This heavy burden of "guilt" has been cited as one of the possible reasons why doctors, as a profession, have one of the highest suicide rates in the country. After much discussion, this particular group of doctors began to see that they had never really made the distinction between their feelings of guilt and those of sorrow or regret or compassion. . . .

*There is a huge difference between feeling **guilty** for something and feeling sorry that it happened or feeling compassion for those who have been hurt. Like these doctors mentioned before, many people carry heavy burdens of guilt because they have not been able to make this distinction in their own lives—either intellectually or emotionally. Sometimes people **feel** guilty when they really are **not** guilty—when they have done their best and have nothing to feel guilty about. There are, of course, other times when people don't feel guilty at all about something that they really **should** feel guilty about, something they have deliberately done to hurt someone.*

***Being** guilty refers to something they have done that they know is morally wrong, that they know will hurt or risk hurting themselves or someone else unnecessarily. People often **feel** guilty, however, not when they have done something deliberately, but when they have tried their best and their best has simply not been good enough or was an honest mistake. On the other hand, feeling sorry that something happened or regretting it does not always mean that people are guilty of causing what has happened. It can simply refer to their ability to feel compassion for those who have been hurt. It is this sense of compassion, this ability to care—to feel with another—that makes them fully human. It does not mean that they have necessarily made a mistake or that they are morally guilty. . . .*

*Ideally, our conscience—what we **think** is right—should be the same as our emotions—what we **feel** is right or what we feel good about. Likewise, our conscience—what we **know** is wrong—should coincide with what we **feel** guilty about. Therefore, we should not **feel** guilty if we have done nothing to **be** guilty for. On the other hand, if we have done something morally wrong, we **should** feel guilty. And, hopefully, out of human compassion, even if we have not caused the hurt, we should feel sorrow and regret at the misfortune of others.*

*Many times during life you will have to assume responsibility for your actions and their consequences. Sometimes this will be for actions which you knew were wrong but did anyway. At those times, it is hoped you will be sensitive enough to the hurt you have caused yourself or others to feel guilty about what you have done—to recognize that it was wrong and to realize that it is something you should not do again. But there will be other times when your actions, although done with a clear conscience, will harm someone. At such times, to the extent that you are human, you should indeed feel sorry and should regret the hurt that results. You should feel compassion for the suffering your actions bring. But you should not **feel** guilty, because you **are not** guilty.*

[A teenage boy] . . . had been driving on a rainy day, with his friend a passenger in the front seat. When he swerved to avoid another car's reckless movement, his car slid into a tree. His friend was seriously injured and confined to the hospital for many months. Every time he went to visit his friend, who was in considerable pain for a long time, he felt guilty and responsible for what had happened.

. . . this boy had not been careless in any way. He had done what he thought was right at the time. He had done the best he could. That was all that he or anybody could have done under the circumstances. What he needed to realize, but found so hard to do, was that he was not responsible in the sense of being guilty for what happened to his friend. But it was certainly understandable that he felt bad about all his friend had to suffer as a result of the accident.

No wonder people's emotions often don't echo their consciences! They are sometimes given false information about morality from ads and television programs. Ads often deliberately attempt (and the people who are in the business of selling products agree) to make people feel, not just bad, but **guilty** *if they don't use such and such a product. Ads educate people to feel guilty about matters which really are not moral concerns.*

On the other hand, ads can be clever manipulators of our sense of right and wrong in the other extreme. Just about anything can be presented as "good for you" without reference to its moral rightness or wrongness. For example, not only is sex often used to promote a product, sexual expression is almost invariably presented as the correct response, usually without mention of a relationship that has progressed to the point of a marriage commitment. Thus the consumer is gradually led to believe (subconsciously perhaps) that sexual expression is good in and of itself without reference to the relationship and that no sexual expression is inappropriate or worthy of guilt. In the end, moral judgment is suspended for the sake of sales. The true manipulation is of persons and their moral sense. . . .

In addition, there is much unnecessary and unjust violence portrayed in the media. It's not difficult to see how, constantly exposed to these influences as we all are today, we would tend to transfer the lessons learned to our moral and emotional responses in our personal lives—lessons which are not only erroneous, but which can cause much human misery as well. . . . That is why it is especially important to distinguish between what you should feel guilty about and what you should not. This can become a crucial factor in how well you will cope with future events.

Michele McCarty, Moral Decision Making for Catholics *(Dubuque, IA: BROWN Publishing-ROA Media).*

Write your answers to these questions on another sheet of paper.

1. Give as many examples as you can from your own life when you have felt guilty about things for which you were not morally responsible. Explain.

2. List as many examples as you can of things that are deliberately intended to make people feel guilty when they really shouldn't feel that way (e.g., TV commercials, things parents say to their children, or ways they treat their children for totally innocent "misbehavior," and so on).

3. How would you feel if you had been the driver of the car in this situation? Why? How would you go about coping with your feelings of responsibility and guilt?

4. Reread **1 John 3:18–24.** What guidance does this passage offer to our formation of conscience?

God Loves Everyone

Readings: **Acts 10:25-26, 34-35, 44-48; 1 John 4:7-10; John 15:9-17**

Imagine God in heaven listening to the prayers of everyone on earth—all these God-seekers speaking to Him from their various religious beliefs. How does it sound to Him? Like bedlam? Or, in some mysterious way, do all these voices in all these languages blend into one?

Cornelius lived in Cesarea, and he was also a God-seeker. Read the story of his faith and his prayer. **Read Acts 10:1–40.**

Why did Peter go to Cornelius house?

What were Peter's words to Cornelius that showed Peter's understanding that God loves everyone?

Below is a list of the major world religions. Match these up with the proper prayer scene.

1. Hinduism   4. Islam   6. Confucianism

2. Judaism   5. Christianity   7. Taoism

3. Buddhism

_____ The dark-skinned men sit shoeless and cross-legged on the floor, wrapped in prayer-shawls. Swaying backwards and forwards, they recite verses from the Torah.

_____ Swami Ramkrishna in his tiny house by the Ganges River will not speak today. He will continue the devotional silence which he began five years ago. Only three days a year does he break the silence.

_____ Yalcin, the Muslim trader at the flea market, will take his prayer rug behind his stand five times today and pray, prostrating himself toward Mecca.

_____ Dai Jo and Lai San, Zen monks in Kyoto, have been up since three this morning and, until eleven tonight, will spend most of the day sitting cross-legged and immovable as they seek to go to the Buddha-nature that lies in the center of their being.

_____ The prayer group meets each morning in the band room. High school students from various denominations gather to read the Bible and to pray together. Even though it lasts only ten minutes, the students who come find it worthwhile.

_____ Before her meeting with the others on the board of directors of the Export House of Ching, Tao Me spent an hour of quiet meditation. She meditated on these Taoists words: "A leader is best when people barely know that he exists . . . of a good leader, who talks little, when his work is done, his aim fulfilled, they will all say, 'We did it ourselves.' "

_____ The China Pearl restaurant was simple and clean. On each of the walls hung scrolls with Chinese script. Each morning before they opened, the Wong family gathered in the kitchen to burn incense before the family shrine. On the wall of the kitchen was this saying:

No lake so still but that it has its wave
No circle so perfect but that it has its blur.
I would change things for you if I could;
As I can't, you must take them as they are.

Read this story by Anthony de Mello:

Jesus at the Football Match

Jesus Christ said he had never been to a football match. So we took him to one, my friends and I. It was a ferocious battle between the Protestant Punchers and the Catholic Crusaders.

The Crusaders scored first. Jesus cheered wildly and threw his hat high up in the air. Then the Punchers scored. And Jesus cheered wildly and threw his hat high up in the air.

This seemed to puzzle the man behind us. He tapped Jesus on the shoulder and asked, "Which side are you shouting for, my good man?"

"Me?" replied Jesus, by now visibly excited by the game. "Oh, I'm not shouting for either side. I'm just here to enjoy the game."

The questioner turned to his neighbor and sneered, "Hmm, an atheist!"

On the way back, we briefed Jesus on the religious situation of the world today. "It's a funny thing about religious people, Lord," we said. "They always seem to think God is on their side and against the people on the other side."

Jesus agreed. "This is why I back people rather than just religions. Religions were made for people, not people for religions."

"You ought to watch your words," one of us said with some concern. "You were crucified once for saying that sort of thing, you know."

"Yes—and by religious people," said Jesus with a wry smile.

Excerpt from The Song of the Bird *by Anthony de Mello, copyright © 1982 by Anthony de Mello, SJ. Used by permission of Doubleday, a division of Bantam, Doubleday, Dell Publishing Group, Inc.*

What do you think is the point of this story? Have you found it to be true in your experience?

_____

_____

_____

_____

_____

_____

Christ with Us

Readings for Ascension: **Acts 1:1-11; Ephesians 1:17-23; Mark 16:15-20**

Readings for Sunday: **Acts 1:15-17, 20-26; 1 John 4:11-16; John 17:11-19**

The important thing about the story of the ascension is not so much that Jesus went to be with the Father. The risen Jesus was always with the Father. This story does tell us that at one point the appearances of Jesus to the early community ceased. Jesus told them to wait and pray for the coming of the Holy Spirit. Perhaps the most important point in the story is the message of the two men dressed in white. "Why are you standing here looking into the skies?" The heavenly messengers were reminding the disciples that they had a task to do.

The disciples knew they had a task, but they did not know how to proceed. They returned to the upper room to pray and wait.

What do you think the disciples talked about in the upper room?

_____

_____

_____

_____

It was only after the ascension that the work of organizing the Church began. Gradually the disciples came to understand what Jesus had intended when he said to Peter, "You are the Rock, and on this Rock I will build my Church." Peter and the other apostles and the others who came to share in their ministry set out to bring the message of Jesus to the whole world. They found ways to preach the gospel to others, to gather the community for worship, to care for the needs of the community, and to bring comfort, healing, and hope to the poor and suffering. Some things worked and some things didn't. Under the guidance of the Holy Spirit, the Church Jesus had founded began to grow and take shape. **Read Acts 1:12–26.**

About how many people were gathered in the upper room? _____

Who were they? _____

_____

Why did the disciples think it was important to choose someone to take the place of Judas? _____

_____

At first the disciples considered themselves to be a reform movement within Judaism. They saw Jesus and his followers as the "new Israel." In order to establish a Jewish community with its own Sanhedrin, or legal body, 120 members were required. Luke reports that there were 120 gathered in the upper room. Just as there were twelve tribes on which the chosen people were founded, now there would be twelve apostles on which the new people of God would be founded.

At first the apostles preached to the Jews, but later they were led by the Holy Spirit to preach to Gentiles as well. At times there were major disagreements among some of the apostles about this issue. They gathered together as a group to pray, to discuss the issue, and to discern the Holy Spirit's direction. This meeting has been called the Council of Jerusalem. Read about this first council in **Acts 15:1–35.**

What was the question before the council? _____

_____

How was it resolved? _____

_____

The early days of the Church are considered normative for the Church. The action of the Holy Spirit through the apostles is considered a standard for the Church for all time. Against this standard we can test the authenticity of our own Christian belief. But we do not simply preserve a memory of what happened long ago. We believe that the Holy Spirit is still working in the Church. The Holy Spirit still works in the members of the Church and in their leaders. The Church continues the task of carrying on the mission of Jesus. The Church still seeks to bring the good news of Jesus to the whole world and seeks to bring into one all those who believe in Jesus.

Name some of the things that Jesus did during his public ministry that the Church continues today.

1. _____

2. _____

3. _____

4. _____

Pentecost

Empowered by the Spirit

Readings: Acts 2:1-11; 1 Corinthians 12:3-7, 12-13; John 20:19-23

The work of the Holy Spirit in the Church and in the individual Christian is one of the mysteries of our faith. We cannot accurately identify or describe the Spirit's work because it is beyond the power of ordinary human language and understanding. In speaking of the work of the Spirit, therefore, we must use the less precise but more powerful language of image and poetry.

The story of the coming of the Spirit upon the Church at Pentecost is told in images of wind, fire, intoxication, and strange languages. The effect of the Spirit is seen in the new courage and eloquence with which the apostles preach the good news.

Our feelings are the mysterious part of us that is hard to put into words. Sometimes it is easier to tell someone else about the experience by telling what it is like. Have you found this to be true? Write about one of **your** feelings that is best communicated through images.

_____

_____

_____

59

Paul wrote to the Galatians to correct some misunderstandings. He described to them the kind of behavior that is evidence of someone who is living by the flesh (focused on self). Then he told them the signs of the working of the Holy Spirit. **Read Galatians 5:22–23.** List below the fruits of the Spirit, the feelings and abilities one has when he or she lives by the power of God's Spirit. Then number them in the order of the most important for you at this time in your life.

_____   _____   _____

_____   _____   _____

_____   _____   _____

In other letters, Paul describes gifts we receive from the Holy Spirit. In the list below, match the gift in Column A with the phrase that describes it in Column B:

Column A

____ Wisdom

____ Reverence

____ Right judgment

____ Wonder and awe in God's presence

____ Understanding

____ Knowledge

____ Courage

Column B

1. Making good decisions

2. Heart-knowledge

3. Following one's convictions no matter what the cost

4. Thinking clearly and understanding the world as it is

5. Recognizing we are always in God's presence

6. Seeing things from all sides

7. Treasuring life and all that sustains it

In 1 Corinthians 12:4–13, Paul tells us that the Holy Spirit gives different gifts to each Christian. The purpose of these gifts is to build up the Body of Christ. These gifts are to be used in ministry to others.

There is a difference between chores or jobs and ministry. Cleaning up after the parish picnic or helping to mow the lawn are part of the responsibility of an adult member of the community. In a way, it is like making your bed. Anybody can do it, once you get to a certain age. Doing it cheerfully is a way of making life in the family more pleasant for everyone.

Ministry is different. Ministry is trying to discover your special talents and gifts. Doing chores in the family and in the Church is one way of beginning to discover your gifts. Helping with religious education classes, for example, you may discover that you have a gift for teaching. Helping with the Church picnic, you may discover that you have a gift for hospitality. Helping with a Church camp, you may discover you have a gift for counseling or for leadership. Helping with the paper drive, you may find that you have a gift for organization and administration.

Think about the chores you have done at home, in school, in clubs, or in your parish. What gifts are you beginning to discover in yourself? How can your gifts be used to continue the mission of Jesus?

_____

_____

Feast of the Holy Trinity

Three Persons in One God

Readings: **Deuteronomy 4:32-34, 39-40; Romans 8:14-17; Matthew 28:16-20**

Jews, Muslims, and Christians believe in the one God who was revealed in the history recorded in the Hebrew Scriptures or Old Testament. While Christians believe in the same God, they believe that God has been revealed even further in their experience of Jesus Christ and His gift of the Spirit. Christians' belief in this Blessed Trinity sets them apart from Jews and Muslims.

Jesus and his disciples were Jews. Every morning they prayed, "Hear, O Israel, the Lord our God is one." Nowhere in the Bible will you find the word Trinity. Why then do Christians count belief in the Trinity as central to Christian faith?

Speaking of God as Father, Son, and Holy Spirit is a way of naming the Christian experience. In coming to know Jesus, the disciples were convinced they were coming to know God in a new way. Jesus spoke of God, the Great Mystery beyond all things, as his Father. John reports that Jesus told his disciples, "The Father and I are one." Jesus taught his disciples to address God as "Abba" in their prayer.

After the resurrection, the disciples experienced the power of the spirit of Jesus in their own lives. They called the spirit they experienced deep within the Spirit of God or the Holy Spirit. But in speaking of God as Father, Son, and Spirit, Christians were not thinking of three gods. Rather, it was the same God they experienced as Father, as Son, and as Holy Spirit. This God, they insisted, is the one God of Abraham, Isaac, and Jacob. This is the God who is mystery, who is the power behind and within all things. This is the God who acted in Jesus Christ to redeem us. This is the God who acts in the Spirit of Love within us.

How would you explain to a Muslim friend that Christians do not believe in three Gods?

_____

_____

_____

_____

There is a legend that St. Patrick used the shamrock to explain the mystery of the Trinity. How would that symbol help your explanation?

_____

_____

61

How God can be three-in-one and one-in-three is a mystery that cannot be fully explained. A mystery, in this sense, is something that eludes the ability of human language and human thought to express. When we talk about the mystery of life, or the mystery of the universe, we are saying that, no matter how much we come to understand about life or about the universe, there is always more to know. Understanding the mystery of God is beyond the capacity of our human minds. Yet that does not mean we can know nothing about God. It means there is always more to know.

What are some things in life you consider a mystery? Tell about one of them here. Why do you call it is a mystery?

_____

_____

_____

If you think you understand the mystery of life or the mystery of God completely, you can be sure of one thing. You are mistaken. In the first few centuries of the Church's history, Christian preachers and teachers tried to find ways to explain their Christian faith to the Greeks. Gradually through much trial and error, Christians agreed on a set of terms to use in talking about the Father, Son, and Holy Spirit as one God. They wanted to be sure to say that there was only one God. But they also wanted to be able to say that there was a distinction among the Father, the Son, and the Holy Spirit. Finally, they decided to talk about the Father, Son, and the Holy Spirit as three *Persons,* three Persons in one God they named the Blessed Trinity.

Corpus Christi
(Solemnity of the
Body and Blood
of Christ)

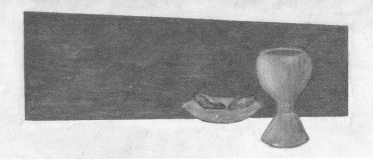

The Body and Blood of Christ

Readings: **Exodus 24:3-8; Hebrews 9:11-15; Mark 14:12-16, 22-26**

Choose one of these two questions and answer it.

1. How is the Mass a meal?

2. How is the Mass a sacrifice?

_____

_____

_____

_____

_____

_____

Chances are you chose to answer question one. While most Catholics have a pretty clear understanding of how the Eucharist is like a meal, they are not so clear on the Eucharist as a sacrifice.

In order to understand what is meant by the Eucharist as sacrifice, it is useful to look at the way we use the term *sacrifice* in our everyday language. The batter hits a "sacrifice fly." The biology student "sacrifices" a frog and dissects it to learn more about living things. Your parents make "sacrifices" so that you can have a college education. You sacrifice your free evening to babysit for your younger brothers and sisters.

In your study of history, you have read about ancient cultures and religions which made a practice of animal sacrifices and even human sacrifice. In the Hebrew Scriptures we read about sacrifices of animals or of grain or other food products offered to God in worship.

Jesus brought a new kind of sacrifice and even, in a sense, went beyond sacrifice as other religions understand it. But the basic idea of sacrifice help us understand the meaning of Jesus' gift of himself to God and to us.

Look up the word *sacrifice* in the dictionary. Write down the various meanings here.

1. _____

2. _____

3. _____

4. _____

5. _____

All of these meanings derive from the original religious meaning of the term *sacrifice*. Where does the term *sacrifice* come from? Literally translated the word means "to make sacred or holy." In sacramental worship (1) a tangible thing (the victim) is chosen to be offered to God; (2) it is killed or destroyed or radically changed (immolation); (3) it is declared to be sacred by certain words or ritual action (consecration); (4) it is consumed so that unity with God can be established or maintained (communion).

Among the most significant events of the Exodus is the establishing of a covenant between Yahweh, the Lord, and Yahweh's chosen people, Israel. This covenant was ratified by a ritual sacrifice. **Read Exodus 24:3–8.** Remember, for ancient peoples, blood represented life. Answer these questions.

Why was blood sprinkled on the altar?

_____

Why was blood sprinkled on the people?

_____

What did the action symbolize about the relationship between God and people?

_____

But the Eucharist is both a sacrifice and a meal. In some ways every meal has a sacrificial element to it. In every meal, life is given and received.

When you are hungry you go in search of food. Food assures you of energy and life. Without food you are condemned to death. When you eat you place the energy found in the food at the service of your own human energy. In fact, when you eat you are always eating a being which has been killed or at least prevented from living. Your life can continue because something else has given its life. The food turns into us. In addition everything we eat is something that could have sustained the life of another being. This is true even of vegetables and fruit, the grain which was to be a seed, an egg which is a potential for new life, or the milk which is meant to nourish the young animal. So, to insure my life and survival, I must take or detract from the life of something else.

The Eucharist is a sacrificial meal in a much deeper sense. In the Eucharist the sacrifice of Jesus' death on the cross is recalled and made present. In receiving the consecrated bread and wine, I nourish myself with the life of the wheat and the grapes which have been "sacrificed" for me. But this bread and wine have become the body of Christ given for me and his blood given for me. It is no longer just the wheat and grapes that give their lives unconsciously for me. No, it is Jesus Christ, sacramentally present, who gives himself voluntarily for me and to me. Now I am in communion with him and live with his life. But rather than Christ being absorbed by me, I become one with the body of Christ.

Now, write a paragraph that answers the question: How is the Eucharist a sacrifice?

_____

_____

_____

_____

_____

_____

Write a prayer of thanksgiving for the many gifts and blessings mentioned in the above quotation.

_____

_____

_____

_____

_____

_____

_____

Jesus Conquers Evil

Readings: **Genesis 3:9-15; 2 Corinthians 4:13-5:1; Mark 3:20-35**

The stories told in Genesis 1-11 were the way the ancient Hebrews explained the meaning of the universe. These stories tell us that the world God created was good. The evil we experience, however, is not God's creation. Evil is often the result of human persons' refusal to serve God, their choice to serve their own self-interest instead of God. The result of their sin can be seen in the alienations or separations we experience. As a result of their sin, there is enmity between the man and the woman, among their children, and even between human beings and the earth and its other creatures.

The choice to serve our own self-interest rather than God is called *sin*. Our sins affect not only ourselves, but the whole human community. Explain how the choice to serve self rather than God is reflected today in:

1. Relationships in families _____

_____

_____

2. Problems in our society _____

_____

_____

3. The condition of the earth and its resources _____

_____

_____

4. Our own personal inner struggles _____

_____

_____

5. Our relationship with God _____

_____

_____

Even as the book of Genesis tells the story of the first sin, it holds out hope. There will be a continuing struggle between the serpent, who represents evil, and the offspring of the woman. (Genesis 3:15) Christian tradition has seen this passage as pointing not only to this continuing struggle, but to a final victory when the head of the serpent is crushed. This final victory is won for us by Jesus Christ, the child of Mary.

Not all the evil in the world can be explained by sin. There are evils we experience which are not the fault of any human person. We think of natural disasters, such as tornadoes and earthquakes. We think of birth defects or of diseases like cancer. Philosophers call these "physical evils," rather than "moral evils." We ask, **Why do bad things happen to good people?**

Write a paragraph describing a situation which leads you to ask this question.

_____

_____

_____

_____

_____

_____

_____

Remember, many of the evils in the world can be explained by sin, but not all evils can be explained in this way. The existence of evil is a mystery, something we can never fully understand. The entire book of Job was written to find some insight into this mystery. Some theologians have offered the explanation that God does not cause the evil, but only permits it. Others have suggested that we ask the wrong question. Since we cannot solve the mystery, we should rather ask, "What am I to learn from this tragedy? What does God want me to do now?" Others point out that Jesus did not offer an elaborate intellectual answer to the mystery of evil. He did something about it. Besides his healing actions in life, he won the victory over sin, the ultimate evil, by his saving death and resurrection.

Throughout his ministry in Palestine, Jesus reached out to those who were suffering. He forgave sins. He healed people who were ill. He taught people to love one another and to forgive one another. Jesus asks us to reach out to others as he did. He asks us to forgive others as he did. He asks us to accept God's love, won for us by his death and resurrection as the cure for our sins and wounds and to bring it to others.

Think about the situation you have described above. In what way can the power of Jesus be brought into that situation?

_____

_____

The Kingdom of God Comes

Readings: **Ezekiel 17:22–24; 2 Corinthians 5:6–10; Mark 4:26–34**

Dag Hammarskjold was secretary-general of the United Nations for many years. He was a man who had known well the horrors of World War II in his native Sweden. As secretary-general, he worked tirelessly to enable nations to settle their differences peacefully. Hammarskjold was killed in 1961 in an airplane crash. After his death, his family and friends discovered his journal. In his journal, Dag Hammarskjold had recorded his struggle for faith. The journal was published some years later as the book, *Markings* (New York: Knopf, 1964).

Following are some statements from Hammarskjold's journal. Choose one of them. Explain what that statement means to you.

1. "The longest journey is the journey inward." (page 58)

   _____

   _____

2. "Pray that your loneliness may spur you into finding something to live for, great enough to die for." (page 85)

   _____

   _____

3. "Never, 'for the sake of peace and quiet,' deny your own experience or convictions." (page 84)

   _____

   _____

4. "Goodness is something so simple: always to live for others, never to seek one's own advantage." (page 89)

   _____

   _____

5. "To say Yes to life is at one and the same time to say Yes to oneself. Yes—even to that element in one which is most unwilling to let itself be transformed from a temptation into a strength." (page 92)

   _____

   _____

6. "Before God, who speaks through all men, you are always in the bottom class in nursery school." (page 104)

   _____

   _____

Check those areas where you feel God's presence—where He is close to you. Prioritize those you have checked (1 is the place where you feel closest).

____ Watching a sunset	____ Climbing a tree
____ During planting time	____ Swimming
____ Helping in the kitchen	____ At a dance
____ Doing dishes	____ Praying
____ Eating	____ Studying
____ At school	____ Reading the Bible

God's kingdom can grow within us as we take time to be quiet, to think and to pray. Use the following meditation to reflect upon the reign of God in your life.

The Lesson

Jesus says, "The Kingdom is like a mustard seed which a man sowed in his field. Mustard is smaller than any other seed but let it grow and it becomes bigger than any garden plant; it is like a tree, big enough for the birds to come and nest among its branches."

I hold this tiniest of seeds
in the hollow of my hand . . .
then I see the full-grown tree it has become,
strong enough to bear the nests of birds.

I move from seed to tree repeatedly in fantasy.

I then observe the seed
through each stage of its growth.

Finally I sit before the full-grown tree
and speak to it:

We talk about the theme of smallness,
the tree and I . . .

About discouragement . . .

risk-taking in our lives . . .

Change and all that it implies . . .
Fruitfulness . . .

Service . . .

And finally,
God's power in our lives.

I end this exercise at Jesus's feet:
I tell him what the mustard tree has taught me
and ask that he will teach me too.

Excerpt from Wellsprings by Anthony de Mello, copyright © 1984 by Anthony de Mello, SJ. Used by permission of Doubleday, a division of Bantam, Doubleday, Dell Publishing Group, Inc.

Write a short homily for your family on the meaning of the parable of the mustard seed.

_____

_____

_____

_____

God's Saving Power

Readings: Job 38:1, 8–11; 2 Corinthians 5:14–17; Mark 4:35–41

Have you ever felt as if you were a small boat about to be dumped over and lost in a swirl of stormy waters? All persons experience times when life seems ready to swamp them, when troubles appear to be more than they can handle. At times like these, our fears make us want to give up. We can become anxious and depressed. But we don't have to do that. We can learn to stay afloat even during very stormy times.

We can begin by asking God's help in realistically reviewing our situation, so that we don't make problems appear worse than they are. We can recognize that God is all-powerful, that He cannot be overcome by any evil, and that He is present with us in time of need. With God's help, we will be able to deal with life's storms rather than be overcome by them.

In each of the clouds, write a word or phrase which summarizes a difficulty you experience in your life today. Below each difficulty, write three ways you might resolve or better cope with the difficulty.

Bible Search

Read each of these Scripture passages: John 14:27, Luke 12:32, Matthew 10:29-31, Luke 11:9-10, John 16:32-33.

Which one offers you the most support for getting through bad times? _____

Why? _____

_____

_____

Music

Is there a song or piece of music which helps you feel better when you are down and out?

Song title: _____

Favorite lines in song: _____

_____

_____

Ad

Read the following classified ad. In the space provided, write a letter of response.

Student, 17, can't take it anymore. Plan to kill self in three weeks. If you think of any reason why I shouldn't, please write. Box 88.

_____

_____

_____

_____

_____

_____

_____

_____

O God,
The waters are rough and my boat is small.
Guide me through stormy waters and bring me safe to shore. Amen.

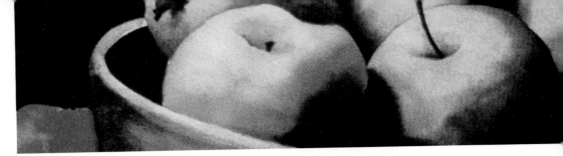

Life Is Precious

Readings: **Wisdom 1:13–15, 2:23–24; 2 Corinthians 8:7, 9, 13–15; Mark 5:21–43**

In nature all living things must change in order to stay alive and grow. In one way or another, nature leaves the old behind and replaces it with new. In the autumn the leaves die and fall; in the spring there is new growth to replace them. The light of the sun fades in the evening, but in the morning it rises again with a new day. The cells of our bodies constantly shed old molecules and absorb new ones. Natural life on earth begins, and it ends, and it begins again. It dies and it rises. Without death, there would be no new life, no growth. And without new life, death, even in nature, would seem final and pointless.

Our inner emotional and spiritual lives reflect the same cycle of dying and rising. Every day, in hundreds of ways, we die a little and we rise a little, or sometimes a great deal. We become depressed, then happy; irritated, then satisfied; tired, then refreshed. There is death, and there is resurrection. This process of dying and rising is the way human life is, and it is something of a mystery to us. We do not want to suffer or die—in any way. That is normal. Yet, at times, we can see why we had to die a little in order to be renewed and changed for the better, in order to grow. At other times we do not fully understand the reasons.

What common experiences make you "die" a little inside? Why?

_____

_____

_____

What common experience makes your spirit rise a little? Why?

_____

_____

_____

Human physical death is even more mysterious to us. It gives us reason to ask many questions. Is this existence truly all there is? Or is there a resurrected life of eternal happiness beyond, as we hope and dream? If so, what does the afterlife hold for us? And, in any event, what do our lives on earth mean?

Then, too, there are life's more tragic mysteries. There is the mystery of pain and suffering, especially of the innocent. We wonder why suffering exists. Sometimes we are emotionally, psychologically, and spiritually left kneeling with Jesus in the garden of his agony, and mentally sweating our own blood as we echo his words: "Please, let this pass." And when it does not, our hearts hang with him on the cross of crucifixion, and we feel like crying out with him: "Why, God, why have You forsaken me?"

List what you think are three of life's most tragic mysteries. Explain why you consider them such.

1. _____

_____

2. _____

_____

3. _____

_____

There is so much about the mystery of suffering that we cannot begin to understand. We are caught up in a mystery greater than ourselves. We question. We wonder whether death or life is the final conclusion and meaning of it all. We seek to understand this mystery more fully as we search for ways of living and coping. This great mystery of life's dying and risings is the same mystery which is at the heart of Christian belief.

Christians choose to believe in a God who understands what we are going through. We believe that, through Jesus, God saved us from meaningless and hopeless suffering. We believe Jesus ultimately came to bring us home to a kingdom of everlasting happiness and joy. It seems obvious from his agony in the garden of Gethsemane the night before he died that Jesus did not want to die painfully any more than we do. But he did want to show us the way to new life. In order to do that, he accepted the fact that he had to suffer and die first. In order to find new life and live more fully, so must we.

Thus Christians believe in a God who became one of us and joined us in the various deaths we must endure in order to show us the way to rising once and for all above them. To our questions on the meaning and the outcome of our suffering and death, Jesus replies: "I am the answer. By my victory over sin and death, your sins are forgiven and your death has been conquered. Trust in my power."

Give an example of a time you have "died," either a little or a lot, and then learned as a result and began to live more fully. Explain. _____

_____

_____

What hope does Christianity promise in the face of life's tragic mysteries? _____

_____

_____

Adapted from Searching *by Michele McCarty (Dubuque, IA: BROWN Publishing–ROA Media, 1984), 210–211.*

Saints Peter and Paul,
June 29

Pillars of Faith

Readings: Acts 12:1-11; 2 Timothy 4:6-8, 17-18; Matthew 16:13-19

St. Michael's Parish had decided to redecorate the parish church. It has been a long time since the parish had redecorated, and Father Sims called a meeting to discuss the project. Mr. and Mrs. Andretti were both planning to go to the meeting. Carol and her older sister Ginger were going to go to a movie.

"Is there anything you'd like to say about the renovation?" Mrs. Andretti asked at the supper table. "I hope they put in air conditioning," said Ginger. "It really gets hot in church during the summer."

"Do you know what I wish they would do?" asked Carol. "I wish they'd take out those big pillars. Sometimes I get behind a pillar and I can't even see the lector or Father Sims."

"That's true," said her father. It depends on where you are sitting. Sometimes you can't see the altar."

"Do you think it's possible to remove the pillars?" Mrs. Andretti asked her husband.

"That depends on whether the pillars are just decorative or if they support the building."

"You mean they can't take them out?" asked Ginger.

"That could be," said her father. "If they are supporting the building, it could be dangerous to remove them."

Name two things a pillar does.

1. _____
2. _____

The Church has always considered Peter and Paul the twin pillars upon which the Church is founded. They are often pictured together, and we celebrate a feast in honor of both of them together. Tell why you think Peter and Paul could be considered "pillars" of the Church.

Peter _____

_____

Paul _____

_____

Peter and Paul did not always agree. One issue on which they had some disagreement was whether Gentile Christians should be required to obey the Jewish ritual laws. In his letter to the Galatians, Paul told about the problem and how it was resolved. **Read Galatians 1:11 through 2:21.**

What gave Paul the assurance that what he taught was true?

_____

_____

How did he describe those who disagreed with him?

_____

Why did he confront Peter? (*Cephas* is Aramaic for Rock, which Peter means in Greek).

_____

73

Why was it important for Paul to check with Peter and the other apostles?

_____

_____

Sometimes people have a childish idea of the meaning of obedience. They think that obedience simply means doing what someone tells you to do. That is usually what it means for children. But adults must be obedient, too. The Scriptures tell us that Jesus was obedient.

The word *obedience* comes from the Latin word *audire,* which means to hear or listen. Obedience means to listen for God's word and then to carry it out. Obedience for an adult cannot simply mean doing whatever one is told. If that were the case, the people who "simply followed orders" at the death camps in Nazi Germany would not be considered criminal. Obedience for an adult must always mean an effort to listen to God's will, as we hear it in Scripture, in the Church, in our families and communities, in the events of our time. It must include an intelligent attempt to understand and a sensitive listening to the Spirit within our own hearts.

Peter can also be seen as a symbol of the official leadership of the Church—the pope and the bishops who are the successors of the apostles. Paul symbolizes the theologian scholars and the charismatic saints throughout the history of the Church who continue to challenge us to be faithful to the faith of the apostles. The task of the theologian is to study, to interpret, and to teach the faith of the apostles. That includes two-way dialogue with the official teachers of the Church to help discern how Church teaching can be faithful to the faith of the apostles and also take into account new knowledge and discoveries. But, like Paul, theologians recognize that it is the bishops and the pope who are the official teachers of the Church.

Finding God in the Ordinary

Readings: **Ezekiel 2:2-5; 2 Corinthians 12:7-10; Mark 6:1-6**

Ezekiel was a priest who lived in the sixth century before Christ. He was one of the group of exiles who were taken to Babylon by Nebuchadnezzar in 597 B.C.E. The exile was a period of great suffering for the Jewish people. At first, those in exile believed that their exile would not last long. They believed that God would not let the temple or the city of Jerusalem be destroyed. But God called Ezekiel to prepare the people for the destruction of Jerusalem and the temple. Ezekiel spoke his prophecy to the exiles even though they did not want to listen to him. Sometimes he acted out God's message in strange, provocative, and even bizarre ways. But the people still did not want to listen to him.

Sometimes we do not like to hear what others have to tell us. Think of times when you made mistakes or poor choices. Think about what you needed to hear. What did you want to hear?

When I	I wanted to hear	I needed to hear
didn't do my homework	_____	_____
stayed out too late	_____	_____
lied	_____	_____
got caught smoking	_____	_____

The first three chapters of the Book of the Prophet Ezekiel describe the call of Ezekiel. **Read Ezekiel's vision in chapter 1.** This chapter uses many symbols to communicate God's message. The cloud and the four living creatures indicate that, even though the temple is destroyed, God is still all-powerful. The wheels which go in all directions at once indicate that God's presence is not limited to just one place. The wheels covered with eyes indicate that, even though the temple would be destroyed, the people could expect that God would see them and be with them even in their place of exile. God is present with His people wherever they are.

Ezekiel is then told to preach to the people, even though they do not want to listen. **Read chapter 2.** Notice that the first reading for this Sunday's liturgy is taken from this chapter. Ezekiel is told to eat a scroll on which are written the terrible things he must tell his fellow exiles. **Read chapter 3.**

Think about someone you know whose task it is to tell people something they do not want to hear. Have you ever had to do this? How did you feel? Write your reflection here.

_____

_____

_____

_____

_____

Jerusalem with its temple was destroyed in 587 B.C.E. Many more of the people of Judah were taken to exile in Babylon. Many of those in exile soon adjusted to their new life and took up the lifestyle of the Babylonians. They no longer practiced their religion. Some thought that, since Jerusalem and the temple had been destroyed, the gods of the Babylonians were surely more powerful than their own God. Others simply busied themselves with their work and living conditions.

But there was a group of the exiles who remained faithful to God. They recognized God's justice in the things that had happened to them. They began to realize that even in their exile they could worship God. Ezekiel's message then became a message of hope. He told them that God would eventually bring them back to their own land. He told them that God was faithful, even though they had been unfaithful. God would create out of them a new people who would be faithful to Him.

Stewardship of the Land

In 1980 the Catholic bishops of the heartland region of the United States wrote a statement to remind their people about their responsibility to care for the land. They opened their statement by saying:

> We are witnessing profound and disturbing changes in rural America. Land ownership is being restructured, agricultural production is becoming more heavily industrialized and concentrated in fewer hands and the earth all too frequently is being subjected to harmful farming, mining and development practices. Such changes are adversely affecting our rural people, their way of life, their land and the wider national and international communities which depend on them to satisfy their hunger. (Strangers and Guests, #1)

The bishops then listed ten principles of land stewardship which come from the Bible and the teaching tradition of the Church.

1. The land is God's.
2. People are God's stewards on the land.
3. The land's benefits are for everyone.
4. The land should be distributed equitably.
5. The land should be conserved and restored.
6. Land use planning must consider social and environmental impacts.
7. Land use should be appropriate to land quality.
8. The land should provide a moderate livelihood.
9. The land's workers should be able to become the land's owners.
10. The land's mineral wealth should be shared.

Choose one of these principles. Write a speech you could give to remind people of how these principles should be lived in your area. What warnings should you give? What hope can you offer? Who will find it hard to listen to this message? Give your speech to your family.

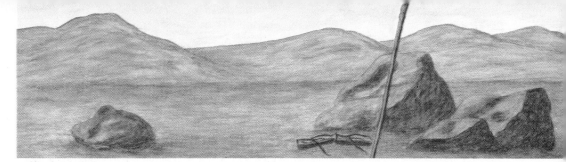

Fifteenth Sunday in
Ordinary Time

Evangelization

Readings: Amos 7:12-15; Ephesians 1:3-14; Mark 6:7-13

How would you answer the following questions?

1. Do you have a personal relationship with Christ?

　＿＿ *Yes*　　＿＿ *No*　　＿＿ *Not sure*

2. Is Jesus Christ the Lord of your life?

　＿＿ *Yes*　　＿＿ *No*　　＿＿ *Not sure*

3. Have you ever had an experience of God in your life that changed you?

　＿＿ *Yes*　　＿＿ *No*　　＿＿ *Not sure*

Evangelization is a word we often associate with Protestants, especially Protestant fundamentalists. We often think of evangelists as preachers on TV or radio. Most of us have been accosted by a fervent evangelist who asked us, "Are you saved?" or at least gave us religious literature. In fact, however, evangelization is a wider Christian concept, deeply rooted in the gospel. Catholics do engage in evangelization. Truly, evangelization is part of our responsibility as confirmed Christians.

But evangelization means more than simply preaching. Pope Paul VI outlined the meaning of evangelization in an encyclical published in 1975. The encyclical was called *On Evangelization in the Modern World.*

Pope Paul outlined different aspects of evangelization. He warned that we should not simply identify evangelization in terms of proclaiming Christ to those who do not know him, even though that is an extremely important aspect of evangelization.

> *Any partial and fragmentary definition which attempts to render the reality of evangelization in all its richness, complexity and dynamism does so only at the risk of impoverishing it and even distorting it. It is impossible to grasp the concept of evangelization unless one tries to keep in view all its essential elements. (#17)*

> *Evangelization is a complex process made up of varied elements: the renewal of humanity, witness, explicit proclamation, inner adherence, entry into the community, acceptance of signs, apostolic initiative. (#24)*

Renewal of Humanity: *Evangelizing means bringing the Good News into all the strata of humanity, and through its influence transforming humanity from within and making it new. (#18)*

For the Church it is a question not only of preaching the Gospel in ever wider geographic areas or to ever greater numbers of people, but also of affecting and as it were upsetting, through the power of the Gospel, mankind's criteria of judgment, determining values, points of interest, lines of thought, sources of inspiration and models of life, which are in contrast with the Word of God and the plan of salvation. (#19)

What are values of young people today that need to be transformed? _____

_____

_____

Witness: *Take a Christian or a handful of Christians who, in the midst of their own community, show their capacity for understanding and acceptance, their sharing of life and destiny with other people, their solidarity with the efforts of all for whatever is noble and good. Let us suppose that, in addition, they radiate in an altogether simple and unaffected way their faith in values that go beyond current values, and their hope in something that is not seen and that one would not dare to imagine. Through this wordless witness these Christians stir up irresistible questions in the hearts of those who see how they live: Why are they like this? Why do they live in this way? What or who is it that inspires them? Why are they in our midst? Such a witness is already a silent proclamation of the Good News and a very powerful and effective one. (#21)*

Do you think anyone would ask these questions about your family? Your parish? _____

_____

_____

Explicit Proclamation: *The Good News proclaimed by the witness of life sooner or later has to be proclaimed by the word of life. There is no true evangelization if the name, the teaching, the life, the promises, the Kingdom and the mystery of Jesus of Nazareth, the Son of God are not proclaimed. (#22)*

Have you ever discussed your faith with anyone who asked? What would you say to a classmate who asked you if

you still go to church? _____

_____

Inner Adherence: *In fact the proclamation only reaches full development when it is listened to, accepted and assimilated, and when it arouses a genuine adherence in the one who has thus received it. An adherence to the truths which the Lord in his mercy has revealed; still more, an adherence to a program of life—a life transformed— which he proposes. (#22)*

It's not just people who don't go to church who need to be evangelized; Catholics themselves need to be

evangelized. Do you agree or disagree? Explain. _____

_____

Entry into the Community: *Such an adherence, which cannot remain abstract and unincarnated, reveals itself concretely by a visible entry into a community of believers. (#23)*

How does your parish provide a warm welcome to newcomers? _____

_____

_____

Acceptance of Signs: *But entry into the ecclesial community will in its turn be expressed through many other signs which prolong and unfold the sign of the Church. In the dynamism of evangelization, a person who accepts the Church as the Word which saves normally translates it into the following sacramental acts: adherence to the Church, and acceptance of the sacraments, which manifest and support this adherence through the grace which they confer. (#23)*

How are adults prepared for baptism in your parish? _____

_____

_____

Apostolic Initiative: *The person who has been evangelized goes on to evangelize others. Here lies the test of the truth, the touchstone of evangelization: it is unthinkable that a person should accept the Word and give himself to the Kingdom without becoming a person who bears witness to it and proclaims it in his turn. (#23)*

How can you evangelize others? _____

_____

The Ministry of Leadership

Readings: **Jeremiah 23:1-6; Ephesians 2:13-18; Mark 6:30-34**

Every parish has the responsibility of meeting the needs of the people in the parish. The parish as a community of faith also has a responsibility to carry on the mission of Jesus in reaching out to others. Here is a list of some of the tasks that must be done in your parish.

1. Preach the gospel.

2. Plan for the celebration of the Eucharist.

3. Minister to the sick and dying.

4. Maintain parish buildings.

5. Educate children and adults in faith.

6. Build a sense of community.

7. Help those who are suffering in any way.

8. _____

9. _____

10. _____

Make a list of the leaders in your parish. Tell which of the above tasks is their responsibility.

Leader	Responsibility
_____	_____
_____	_____
_____	_____
_____	_____
_____	_____

Each one of us has special gifts. Through baptism, each of us is called to use our gifts in the ministry of the Christian community. Some people are called to the ordained ministry in the Church. They will serve as bishops, priests, or deacons. Others are called to religious communities. They will make public vows in the Church and will serve in various Church ministries. Most Christians are lay people. Lay people sometimes serve in full-time ministries within the Church. Some may serve in Church ministries in their free time. All are to live out the call to be a servant by their lives.

Check the ministries below that you think you would find interesting.

___ Lector—reads at the community celebration of Eucharist

___ Eucharistic minister—ministers the Eucharist to people at Mass or to the sick in their homes

___ Youth minister—helps young people in the parish to grow in faith

___ Parish council member—helps the pastor plan how the parish can meet the needs of its members

___ Hospital chaplain—helps sick people and their families to deal with illness

___ Social service minister—helps the poor and needy in the name of the Church

___ Social justice advocate—works to change unjust social structures

___ Communications—seeks to spread the gospel through the use of television, radio, newspapers, books, and magazines

___ Administration—helps the Church to organize and carry out its work effectively

___ Peer ministry—reaches out to friends and peers who need someone to listen to them

Look up information about one of the following. Explain how Christians minister through these organizations.

Campaign for Human Development

National Catholic Rural Life Conference

National Council of Catholic Women

Knights of Columbus

Bread for the World

Pax Christi

_____

_____

_____

_____

_____

_____

_____

_____

_____

_____

_____

_____

_____

Seventeenth Sunday
in Ordinary Time

Eucharist as Meal

Readings: **2 Kings 4:42–44; Ephesians 4:1–6; John 6:1–15**

Catholics believe that the Eucharistic celebration is a holy meal which recalls the Last Supper, reminds us of our unity with one another in Christ, and anticipates the banquet of God's kingdom. The Eucharist is the Christian community's celebration meal.

Think of five ways that a family celebration meal is like the Eucharist.

Family Meal

1. _____
   _____
2. _____
   _____
3. _____
   _____
4. _____
   _____
5. _____
   _____

Eucharist

1. _____
   _____
2. _____
   _____
3. _____
   _____
4. _____
   _____
5. _____
   _____

81

For Reflection

Truly partaking of the body of the Lord in the breaking of the Eucharistic bread, we are taken up into communion with Him and with one another. "Because the bread is one, we though many, are one body, all of us who partake of the one bread" (1 Corinthians 10:17). In this way all of us are made members of His body (cf. 1 Corinthians 12:27), "but severally members one of another" (Romans 12:5).

As all the members of the human body, though they are many, form one body, so also are the faithful in Christ (cf. 1 Corinthians 12:12). Also, in the building up of Christ's body there is a flourishing variety of members and functions. There is only one Spirit who, according to His own richness and the needs of the ministries, distributes His different gifts for the welfare of the Church (cf. 1 Corinthians 12:1–11). (Dogmatic Constitution on the Church, number 7)

Imagine that, while walking along, you met someone hungry or homeless. What could you do to help? Write about it here.

1. One day, while walking . . .

   _____
   _____
   _____
   _____
   _____
   _____

2. Now write what you would most likely do if this really happened.

   _____
   _____
   _____
   _____
   _____
   _____

3. Are your responses the same for both 1 and 2? If not, what stands in the way?

   _____
   _____
   _____
   _____
   _____
   _____

Take action!

- If you have hunger walks in your area to raise money for the needy, plan to take part in it. If you do not, gather together with some friends and plan an organized activity to raise money for the poor.

- If you earn any money, think about putting some of it in the collection on Sunday to help those in need.

- Identify one thing you could do this week that will help someone else and follow up on it.

Eighteenth Sunday in
Ordinary Time

Bread of Life

Readings: **Exodus 16:2-4, 12-15; Ephesians 4:17, 20-24; John 6:24-35**

Reread Exodus 16:2-15. Why were the people complaining?

_____

_____

What did they see as the solution to their problems? _____

_____

What did God do for them? _____

_____

The Israelites thought that God had abandoned them. Sometimes we also feel that God has abandoned us. Make a list of problems that we face today.

Personal	**Community**	**World**
_____	_____	_____
_____	_____	_____
_____	_____	_____

God has promised to be with us on our life's journey. He has promised to give us what we need. He will be our Bread of Life.

How can relying on God help us to face our problems?

_____

_____

_____

Someone has said that God's plan for solving the problems of the world is to get people to sit down at a meal together. Once people have gathered around a table and relaxed, shared food and ideas, conversation and funny stories, they will be more ready to talk about and settle their problems. In fact, both the prophets and Jesus himself often used the image of a meal to describe the kingdom of heaven.

Look up **Isaiah 55:1-3.** What does the image of the meal in this passage tell you about the kingdom of heaven?

_____

_____

_____

_____

Look up the following passages in the Gospel according to Luke. Write the Scripture reference next to the sentence that states a characteristic of the kingdom described in that passage.

Luke 10:38-42   Luke 14:1-11

Luke 14:15-24   Luke 16:19-31

Luke 15:11-31   Luke 19:1-10

_____ Jesus reaches out to all, even those everyone considers to be sinners.

_____ Those who close their hearts to the poor and hungry cannot enter the kingdom.

_____ Men and women are equally called to the kingdom.

_____ God invites everyone into His kingdom.

_____ God calls us to rejoice in every sinner who repents.

_____ The kingdom of God is for those who are humble.

Read Matthew 26:17-35. At the Last Supper, Jesus gathered his friends together for a meal, as he had done so many times before. But this time was different. He knew what awaited him the next day. He also knew that he could still back out of it.

At the Eucharist, we remember that Jesus chose to remain faithful to his Father, even though he knew what awaited him. It is this decision that we celebrate at Eucharist. In celebrating the Eucharist, we come to share in the power of his decision to give himself in loving trust of his Father. In our celebration of the Eucharist, we, too, are strengthened to give ourselves for others as Jesus did.

What do you think of the statement that God's solution to the problems of the world is to get people to sit down at table together?

_____

_____

How can Christians' celebration of the Eucharist help to solve the problems of the world?

_____

_____

God Is with Us

Readings: **Daniel 7:9-10, 13-14; 2 Peter 1:16-19; Cycle A: Matthew 17:1-9, Cycle B: Mark 9:2-10, Cycle C: Luke 9:28-36**

You have heard about Jesus since you were a little child. You have probably formed some opinions about what Jesus is like, whether you realize it or not. Some of these opinions may be based in the Scriptures and some may not.

Some people have developed false beliefs about Jesus that may turn a lot of people away from him. Jesus has been depicted in some Christian art and in some Christian preaching as effeminate and overly pious. Tell why each of the following images of Jesus is false.

Jesus the Superstar _____

_____

Jesus as Superman _____

_____

Jesus as Security Blanket _____

_____

Even in the early years of the Church there were misunderstandings about Jesus. Christians teachers tried to find ways to help Christians understand who Jesus was. The stories which have been collected in the Gospels were often told with that purpose in mind. Today's story about Jesus' transfiguration may have been such a story. It helped them to explain that Jesus is God's beloved Son. It also helped them to explain that Jesus was the Messiah. Jesus is the one who fulfills the Law, represented by Moses, and the prophets, represented by Elijah.

And it took a while before the early Christians understood what it meant to call Jesus God's Son. Like Christians, Jews have a strong belief that there is only one God. The Jews had to make a great deal of effort to hold on to that belief because most of their neighbors believed in many gods. If Christians called Jesus the Son of God, Jews wondered if they were saying that there was more than one God. The Jews would normally interpret the term "son of God" in a more general sense as meaning one who was devoted to God. They did not mean to say that that person was divine. But Christians did mean that Jesus was divine.

People are naturally inquisitive. They want to know more. Notice, for example, how magazines and television tries to tell us more and more about our national leaders or about our favorite actors and actresses or rock stars. The early Christians were no different. They wanted to understand what it meant to say that Jesus was the Son of God. Many pastors and teachers looked for ways to explain who Jesus was.

Christian missionaries soon began to bring the gospel to people who were not Jews. These people had other religious traditions. The missionaries and teachers tried to find ways of explaining who Jesus was. They needed to find ways that the people would understand. They also needed to find ways that were in continuity with the Scriptures.

Sometimes the explanations offered by pastors, teachers, and missionaries were very helpful and helped Christians to better understand the Scriptures. However, there were other explanations that did not go along with what Christians traditionally believed about Jesus. It became necessary for the Church to clarify what the true teaching about Jesus was. They also needed to identify false teaching, or heresy.

One explanation was offered by the Docetists in the first century. They taught that the Son of God only appeared to be a man in Jesus Christ. Even though his body appeared real, they said, actually it was just a ghost. For them, it was impossible that God could experience hunger and thirst, fear, suffering and death. So, they said, he only appeared to do so. The problem with this explanation is, first of all, that it does not agree with the Scriptures or Christian belief and tradition.

Write **John 1:14** here. _____

_____

_____

Find two other examples in the Gospels that show that the disciples experienced a truly human Jesus. Write the references here.

1. _____ 2. _____

Arius was a popular preacher in Alexandria. Arius tried to help people understand who Jesus was. Arius believed that Jesus was really God's Son, but he did not believe that the Son of God was equal to the Father. He said that the Father existed before the Son. He said that Jesus Christ is God's greatest creature. For Arius, Jesus Christ was not God made human.

The teaching of Arius attracted many followers, but it was not true to the gospel. If Jesus Christ is not divine, by what power can he redeem us from our sins?

Controversy about correct teaching continued through the first seven centuries of the Church's existence. In order to clarify the Church's teaching, several meetings of the bishops of the Church were held. There were called ecumenical (or worldwide) councils. The most important of these official ecumenical councils were held in Nicea in 325, in Constantinople in 381 and again in 680-681, in Ephesus in 431, and in Chalcedon in 451. Through these councils, the Church's teaching about who Jesus is was clarified. Churches which do not accept these councils are not considered Christian, however good they may be.

The Creed we proclaim every Sunday is the official statement which was approved during these councils. We believe that Jesus Christ is both divine and human. We believe that the Son of God is equal to the Father. We also believe that Jesus Christ is truly human. Although we can never fully explain the mystery of how this can be, we affirm this as the truth about Jesus.

Write three phrases from the Nicene Creed which reflect our belief in the divinity of Jesus.

_____

_____

_____

Write three phrases from the Nicene Creed which reflect our belief in the humanity of Jesus.

_____

_____

_____

Sharing God's Life

Readings: 1 Kings 19:4–8; Ephesians 4:30–5:2; John 6:41–51

Mary walked home slowly. She had a great deal to think about. This had been her first day at her new summer job at Pleasant Hill. In many ways it had been a confusing day. There were so many new things to learn. It was hard to remember all the residents' names and the names of the nurses and staff.

The nursing home itself was not new to Mary. She had often come with her mother to visit her great grandmother at the nursing home before Gram had died last summer. In that sense, she had known what to expect. What had struck Mary this day, however, was the response she had received when she went into Mrs. O'Malley's room. She had just come from Mrs. Sullivan's room. Mrs. Sullivan was very sad and depressed. She just wanted to die.

"I'm fine," Mrs. O'Malley had said in response to Mary's query. She had drawn Mary's attention to the birds outside her window. "Life is a gift," she had said to Mary. "Every day is a gift."

What are some things that might make you see life as a burden?

_____

_____

_____

_____

_____

What are some things that might help you to see life as a gift?

_____

_____

_____

_____

If we see life as a gift, how does it affect the way we relate to others?

_____

_____

_____

_____

Life is God's greatest gift to us. God gives us the gift of life so that we can know and love Him and share that love with one another. Jesus shows us how to live life as a gift from God. When he met people who were sick or alienated, he reached out to them. He wanted to heal them and welcome them into his friendship.

Look up the following Scripture passages. Write the sentence that tells what Jesus desires for his people.

John 10:10 _____

_____

John 15:11 _____

_____

Jesus often took time to give thanks to God for His gifts. Even at the Last Supper, as Jesus faced the certainty of his suffering and death, he gave thanks to God. **Read Matthew 26:26–27.**

After the resurrection, when the first Christians gathered to "break bread" in memory of Jesus, they called their gathering *eucharist,* a word that means "thanksgiving." At the Eucharist we celebrate God's gift of life to us. We thank God for the gift of life and the gift of grace, our friendship with God. As we are nourished with the Eucharist, we offer our own lives in thanksgiving to God. We commit ourselves to live our lives fully and to help others to live their lives fully.

Reread the second reading for this Sunday, **Ephesians 4:30–5:2.** Write a homily on this passage. Write the homily as if it were addressed either to your classmates or to the community with which you usually worship on Sunday. Remember, a homily expands on the Scripture reading. It helps people to see what the Scripture can mean in their lives. Tell how participating in the Eucharist can help people live their lives fully.

_____

_____

_____

_____

_____

_____

_____

_____

_____

_____

_____

_____

_____

_____

_____

_____

Twentieth Sunday in
Ordinary Time

Jesus Is Present in the Eucharist

Readings: **Proverbs 9:1–6; Ephesians 5:15–20; John 6:51–58**

Customs are ways of showing respect to another person. What are customs people observe in your community to acknowledge others or to show respect to them? (e.g. men remove their hats in church; we wave or nod to someone we meet on the street)

_____

_____

_____

Catholic Christians have customs and rituals which show our respect for the Blessed Sacrament. How would you explain the following rituals to someone who is not a Catholic?

Genuflecting before going into your pew _____

_____

_____

_____

_____

Keeping a sanctuary lamp burning near
the tabernacle _____

_____

_____

_____

Benediction _____

_____

_____

The following is an instruction taken from the writings of Cyril, a fourth century bishop of Jerusalem.

When you approach, do not go stretching out your open hands or having your fingers spread out, but make the left hand into a throne for the right which shall receive the King, and then cup your open hand and take the Body of Christ, saying over it Amen. . . .

Then after you have partaken of the Body of Christ, approach the chalice with the Blood without stretching out your hands, but bowed, in a position of worship and reverence, and repeat the Amen and sanctify yourself by receiving the Blood of Christ.

The practice of receiving communion on the tongue arose in the late ninth century. Some historical evidence suggests that the practice arose to prevent poorly instructed persons from taking the Eucharist home to use in superstitious ways. Other indications suggest that the practice developed to distinguish lay persons from clergy. It was at about the same time that the practice of not allowing lay persons to receive from the cup arose.

The reform of the liturgy begun by the bishops at Vatican II (1962-1965) has restored the practice of receiving communion in the hand. It has also encouraged extending the cup to the laity. Some Catholics still prefer to receive communion according to the custom which developed in the ninth century. Which method do you prefer? Why?

_____

_____

_____

From the early days of the Church, theologians have tried to find ways to explain what Jesus did the night of his Last Supper. Sharing a meal has a special meaning for people. At the Last Supper, Jesus not only extended that meaning, but he transformed the meaning of the bread and wine he shared with them.

To describe this change in meaning, the official Church teachings use the term *transubstantiation.* This means that the reality of the bread and wine, its substance, what makes it bread or wine, is changed into the body and blood of Christ. Although the appearances of the bread and wine—their color, shape, taste, etc., and their other physical and chemical properties—remain the same, faith tells us that what we eat and drink is the body and blood of Jesus. In giving us the Eucharist, Jesus gives us not just a sign or proof of his love, he gives us himself.

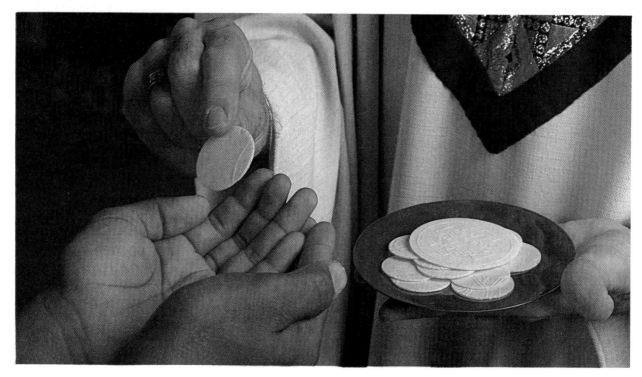

Eucharist: A Covenant of Love

Readings: Joshua 24:1-2, 15-18; Ephesians 5:21-32; John 6:60-69

Jeanne practiced her flute solo one more time. She wanted it to be perfect. This solo would be her part in the celebration of her grandparents' golden wedding anniversary. On the fifteenth of October, John and Alice Keanne would celebrate with their family and friends the gift of their fifty years together.

The whole family had helped to plan this celebration. Aunt Kate and Aunt Helen had written a short story of the family's history and illustrated it with snapshots from Grandmother's collection. Uncle Steve was planning a slide show of pictures he had chosen to present in the afternoon. The whole family would enjoy Steve's storytelling. Aunt Ellen and Uncle Ted were in charge of the dinner. Uncle Ray's band would play for the dance in the evening. Jeanne was part of the liturgy committee that had worked with Father Mike to prepare the Mass. The whole family was looking forward to a grand celebration.

John and Alice Keanne stood before the altar. In response to Father Mike's questions, they renewed the covenant they had made fifty years ago. They renewed their promise to love and cherish one another "in good times and in bad, in sickness and in health, all the days of our lives."

"John and Alice are an important sign to this community," Father Mike told the people who came to celebrate. "They are a sign of faithful love, the kind of love God has for His people. Fifty years ago John and Alice made a covenant with each other before God. They promised to love one another with the kind of love with which Christ loves us. We, their family, friends, and neighbors, have come to know God better because we have known John and Alice."

How does your family celebrate wedding anniversaries?

_____

_____

_____

Think of married couples you know. Below are listed some qualities of God's love. After each quality write the name of a couple who helps the community better understand that aspect of God's love.

compassionate _____

welcoming _____

generous _____

forgiving _____

faithful _____

A covenant is a sacred bond established between two parties. It is different from a partnership because a partnership involves terms and limits which we set down for a specified period of time, short term or long term. Unlike a contract, which often includes qualifying clauses and riders, a covenant involves the whole person. While a partnership may be simply a private affair, a covenant involves the wider community. A covenant changes the relationship of the persons to one another and of the couple to the society. For persons of faith, the marriage covenant is centered upon God. Those who enter into the covenant know that God is present within their relationship, strengthening and supporting them.

Each of us entered into a covenant with God at our baptism. We promised to love God and to live as God's sons and daughters. The covenant is a love bond like the marriage covenant. We renew our covenant of love with God every time we celebrate the Eucharist. When we receive Holy Communion we are promising to love God above all things and our neighbor as ourselves. In Holy Communion Jesus gives us the strength to love as he has loved us.

Reread the second reading for this Sunday's liturgy, **Ephesians 5:21–32.** What are two ways the love of husband and wife is like the love between Christ and the Church?

1. _____

_____

2. _____

_____

Reread the gospel selection for this Sunday, **John 6:60–69.** Write the words of Peter which express his commitment of faith.

_____

_____

_____

Write the words of Peter on a card and post it in your room. Memorize them as your own act of faith.

The Spirit of the Law

Readings: **Deuteronomy 4:1–2, 6–8; James 1:17–18, 21–22, 27; Mark 7:1–8, 14–15, 21–23**

Forming a conscience is a very important part of maturing into adulthood. Conscience is more than the "little voice inside you." It includes a general awareness of what is right and what is wrong. It is a set of values and principles that guides your judgments. This set of values and principles continues to grow and expand as you have more experiences. Conscience is also the ability to make decisions according to your values and principles in a given case. Finally conscience includes the drive to follow your best moral judgment.

As you move toward adulthood, you are more responsible for your decisions. Complete the following. Check all those that apply to you. Extra space is allowed for those not included in the list.

People I admire—pattern my life after	Persons whose opinions I seek when making decisions	Sources of information I rely on when making decisions
sports hero	best friend	favorite magazine
grandparent	older brother or sister	Scripture
patron saint	teacher or counselor	TV
Jesus	priest	religion class
parent	God through prayer	movies
favorite saint	parent	
uncle or aunt	friend's parent	
TV star	adult friend	
movie star	steady boyfriend or girlfriend	
politician		
teacher		
older brother or sister		

Circle the person or source in each category that is **most important to you.** Put an "X" by the persons or sources which reflect God's law of love.

Decisions can be based on such things as feelings, thoughts, past actions, or the influence of other people. Right decisions are rooted in a knowledge of God's Law, and an understanding of how it addresses my life. Each person is responsible for the formation of his or her conscience. Conscience is formed in response to how God's Law and life have touched our hearts.

Consider a time when you failed to respond in a loving way toward someone. What happened? What factors influenced your action? What other choices could you have made?

_____

_____

_____

_____

When we are younger, we tend to think that someone else makes laws for us to obey. We do not always understand the reasons for the rules and laws. Parents, of course, make rules for their children which they think will be for their good. As we mature, we realize that authorities makes laws or rules for the common good. The Church teaches moral principles which point out a way to live in harmony with God and other people. But it is up to the individual to adopt these principles as her or his own.

Forming our conscience is a continuing task for a Christian. As new situations arise, we need to discover ethical principles which can guide our actions. Fifty years ago, people did not need principles to govern the use of nuclear power or genetic manipulation. At this time in your life, you may not need to know the moral principles which govern the world of finance or the principles of a just war. But, as you continue to have new experiences, you will need to develop your conscience so that you will be able to make judgments about the situations which you will face.

Prayer, reading and reflecting on Scripture, listening to the weekly homily, reading your diocesan newspaper or other religious periodicals, and discussing the issues with other Christians are all ways you can discover the principles that will guide your judgments.

Reread the readings for the Twenty-Second Sunday in Ordinary Time. What principles do they offer which can guide your judgments?

Deuteronomy 4:1-2, 6-8 _____

_____

James 1:17-18, 21-22, 27 _____

_____

Mark 7:1-8; 14-15, 21-23 _____

_____

Moses told the people that God would stay close to them if they would call upon Him. God was the source of their strength. Jesus invited the people to call God "Abba," to believe that God loved them dearly and that God was the source of their strength. Today we are strengthened by God through prayer, Scripture, and the Eucharist. However, we must be open to hear God.

Take time for a centering prayer. Find a comfortable, quiet place. Relax in a comfortable position. Let the tension and worry flow out of your body as you take slow, easy, deep breaths. Feel the support and strength of the earth beneath you. As you continue to take deep, slow breaths, share with God your thoughts, feelings, and concerns. Relax and find peace in the presence of the Lord.

Take time for prayer when you are faced with a difficult decision.

Twenty-Third Sunday
in Ordinary Time

Open to God

Readings: Isaiah 35:4–7; James 2:1–5; Mark 7:31–37

It's Not Just Us, It's Justice

Justice is love's absolute minimum. Yet we know that the reality of life is that many people suffer injustice. Each of us has a responsibility for the formation of our social conscience. This means we have a stake in all people's lives because all of us are God's creation. Using the AAAR model, reflect on your life.

Awareness. Where do I see prejudice in my life—in my family, in me, at school, with friends, in my town?

_____

_____

_____

_____

Analysis. What has created the prejudice? Do I believe I have a responsibility toward all people? What does Jesus say about how we are to treat people?

_____

_____

_____

_____

Action. How must I change to eliminate prejudice? Am I willing to change? How can I help to create an awareness in my family, my friends, my school, my town? What values are the basis for my action?

_____

_____

_____

_____

Reflection/Reorientation. What have I learned? Where do I go from here?

_____

_____

_____

_____

The choice of sin occurs in the human heart, and sin is expressed through personal choices and actions. But it has social consequences. Sin is expressed in some of the structures of human communities. Sinful structures are not simply imperfect human organizations; rather, such structures involve a systematic abuse of the rights of certain groups or individuals. The sinfulness lies in the unjust way in which social relationships are organized. An extreme example is institutionalized racial or ethnic segregation; a less striking example is the absence or inadequacy of minimum wage laws. A very contemporary example is the imbalance in the distribution of the world's goods, which calls for a new international economic order.

Responsibility for correcting a situation of "social sin" rests upon all who participate in the society in question: those whose rights are being systematically denied are called to assert them; others are called to seek to change existing patterns of social relationships.

"Social sin" can affect such large numbers of people that it is almost impossible to identify its causes. It can be so deeply rooted as almost to defy eradication. It can be the fault of so many that no one in particular can be held to blame. But precisely because social injustices are so complex, one must resist the temptation to think that there is no remedy for them. (Sharing the Light of Faith, #165)

Choose one of the following situations. Tell why it can be called a situation of social sin. Whose rights are being violated? What social structures support this situation?

1. Apartheid in South Africa

2. Dangers of pesticides for migrant farm workers

3. Destruction of rain forests in Brazil

4. Drug problems in the United States

5. Abuse of land

6. Poisoning of the environment

7. Abortion

_____

_____

_____

_____

_____

_____

_____

_____

_____

_____

Music: "Jesus Loves the Little Children," "One Bread, One Body," "What You See in the Dark" (*Glory & Praise*), "It's Wrong" (Stevie Wonder), "Russians" (Sting).

Prayer

Creator God,

Open my ears that I may hear Your word.

Open my eyes that I may see You in all people.

Open my heart that I may live Your love.

Faith in Action

Readings: **Isaiah 50:5-9; James 2:14-18; Mark 8:27-35**

Today's lesson is intended to be an experience in prayer, in deepening your relationship with Jesus Christ. Read the following meditation slowly and thoughtfully. Writing your answers in a private journal can help you learn to meditate. Begin by finding a quiet place where you can be attentive to God. A lighted candle, a cross, or a picture of Jesus may help to focus your attention. Spend some time in quiet before you begin.

> *I think of the impact Jesus Christ has had on human history . . .*
>
> *and on my life . . .*
>
> *I tell him what it is about him that appeals to me the most.*
> *I listen to what he says in reply.*
>
> *I tell him which of his words have had the greatest impact on me*
> *and how those words have influenced my life.*
>
> *His disciples sometimes speak of his presence in their lives.*
> *I ponder on the meaning that word "presence" has for me.*
> *In what way, if at all, has he been present in my past and in my life today?*
>
> *He indicated he was sent to teach us how to love. What kind of love has Jesus taught me?*
> *If I am a loving person, to what extent is he responsible?*
>
> *He also claimed he was sent to bring liberation to the lives of people.*
>
> *Has this been my experience?*
> *Or have I, on the contrary, felt constricted and oppressed*
> *by his demands and teachings?*
> *Or have I experienced both oppression and liberation simultaneously?*
> *In what specific areas?*
>
> *Before I end my dialogue, I ask myself what impact Jesus had on yesterday.*
>
> *And I tell him what I think his influence will be on what I think and say and do today.*

What impact do you think Jesus Christ has had on history?

_____

_____

_____

What appeals to you most about Jesus?

_____

_____

Which of Jesus' words do you think have had the greatest impact on you?

_____

_____

_____

As Peter listened to Jesus, he became upset. He didn't want to hear that Jesus was going to suffer or that he, Peter, would have to suffer. He anticipated a more comfortable life. It was a time of breakdown for Peter. Jesus was trying to tell Peter that serving others and growing through the pain and difficult times was the only way to have life. Such growth is a breakthrough. We grow in a personal relationship with Jesus.

Become the person God invites us to be. Find true happiness and meaning in life.

Consider the times of growth and change in your life. Name a time of breakdown—a time when you knew pain or didn't want to follow through. Name the breakthrough that followed. As you look back, how did you grow through that experience? What did you learn?

Breakdown   **Breakthrough**

_____   _____

_____   _____

_____   _____

Triumph of the Cross,
September 14

The Cross of Salvation

Readings: **Numbers 21:4-9; Philippians 2:6-11; John 3:13-17**

Write some things you know about the historical Jesus (the Jesus born in Bethlehem, lost in the temple in Jerusalem, dying on a cross outside the gates of Jerusalem).

_____

_____

_____

_____

_____

Write some things you know about the resurrected Jesus.

_____

_____

_____

_____

_____

The Gospel writers and the first communities of believers talked and wrote about the historical Jesus after they had experienced Jesus' resurrection. It is almost impossible to separate the historical Jesus from the resurrected Christ. The first Christians called their Savior _Jesus, the Christ._ We now say Jesus Christ.

The first Christians, followers of Jesus Christ, recalled Jesus' words and actions and tried to live as Jesus had taught them to live. They felt the strength of the resurrected Christ working through them. They often found that, like Jesus, they, too, had to give their lives for the sake of the gospel.

St. Andrew died on a cross. An old tradition says that Andrew was crucified on an X-shaped cross. We sometimes call an X a "St. Andrew's cross."

St. Peter died upside down on a cross like Jesus' cross.

X

+

Write some beliefs that gave them strength to live and die as Jesus did.

_____

_____

99

How do you, as a Christian, bring the risen Jesus to our world today?

_____

_____

Why does belief in God's love for everyone sometimes require suffering and death from followers of Jesus?

_____

_____

Think of people in our times who suffered and died for their beliefs.

Archbishop Oscar Romero spoke out against the powerful people of San Salvador who oppressed the poor. He was shot to death while offering Mass on March 24, 1980.

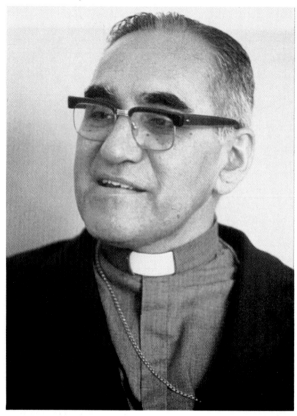

On December 2, 1980, Sisters Maura Clarke, MM, Ita Ford, MM, Dorothy Kazel, OSU, and lay missioner Jean Donovan were killed in El Salvador. They were missionaries helping the people hear Jesus' good news that everyone has dignity, is created and loved by their God.

Say the following prayer and think about the meaning of the words for you today.

> _Lord, by your cross and resurrection,_
> _you have set us free._
> _You are the Savior of the world._

Twenty-Fifth Sunday
in Ordinary Time

Power and Powerlessness

Readings: Wisdom 2:12, 17-20; James 3:16-4:3; Mark 9:30-37

What are your thoughts and feelings when you read the following sayings of Jesus?

"If anyone wishes to rank first, he must remain the last one of all and the servant of all." (Mark 9:35)

_____
_____
_____
_____

"Love your enemies and pray for those who persecute you." (Matthew 5:44)

_____
_____
_____
_____

"Offer no resistance to injury. When a person strikes you on the right cheek, turn and offer him the other also." (Mark 5:39)

_____
_____
_____
_____

"There is no greater love than this: to lay down one's life for one's friends." (Matthew 15:13)

_____
_____
_____
_____

The early Christian community seemed to understand these sayings of Jesus to require absolute nonviolence. Early Church teachers (known to later generations as *the Fathers)* emphasized that Christians should not harm others, even if they were harmed. Even though they suffered many persecutions under the Roman emperors, the Christians never resisted with violence. They gave witness to the power of the Spirit within them by forgiving those who were persecuting them. During this period, Christians were not allowed to become soldiers. Any soldier who wanted to become a Christian had to leave the army.

When Christianity was legalized in the Roman Empire in 413, the situation changed. Christianity became the religion of the Empire, but there was still some debate about whether Christians could be involved in the military. Many Christians continued to maintain the earlier tradition and argue that Christians may not use violence against others.

But another tradition developed in the Church because the Empire needed to defend itself against invaders. Some Christians began to argue that in some situations it was good and proper to wage a war. They reminded people that Jesus said, "There is no greater love than this, to lay down one's life for one's friends." (Matthew 15:13) Defending an innocent person, they argued, might be such a situation.

In time, Christian theologians worked out criteria by which a particular war as being just. This just war theory has guided Christians through the centuries.

When Is a War a Just War?

In order for a war to be considered just, it must fulfill certain criteria.

1. War is permissible only to confront a real and certain danger. Protecting innocent life or preserving conditions necessary for decent human existence might be such dangers. A war of revenge is never justified.

2. The decision for war must be made by those with the responsibility for public order. Private groups or individuals may not make this decision.

3. Do the rights and values involved justify killing? Is justice really on our side? This is a very difficult criteria. We like to think God is on our side. Every government will try to make the case that they are in the right.

4. The intention of the war must be for a just cause and not for other reasons. There must always be an effort at reaching reconciliation and peace. There should be no unnecessary destructive acts or unreasonable conditions like unconditional surrender.

5. There must be a reasonable chance of success. If there is no reasonable way you can achieve justice through this war, the war is not justifiable.

6. The good to be achieved must outweigh the evil that will result from it. The effect of the war on the country and on the world community must be considered. What will the war do to our enemies, our allies, our own country? How many will die, be injured, or lose their homes? It is not moral to "destroy a city in order to save it."

7. The war must be waged according to the principles of natural law and international law. Some means of warfare are so horrendous that they have been outlawed by agreement among nations. Wanton violence, looting, massacre, torturing of prisoners are outlawed.

Many Christians today ask, "In a time when the means of war are so destructive, is it possible to have a just war?"

Interview several adults and young people in your family, school, or community. Try to find out what they think a just war is. What do they think Jesus would say about their approach? How does their criteria compare to the Church's just war theory? Report your findings here.

_____

_____

_____

_____

_____

_____

_____

_____

_____

Ecumenism

Readings: Numbers 11:25-29; James 5:1-6; Mark 9:38-43, 45, 47-48

While the Spirit cannot be physically seen, the actions of the Spirit are apparent. Persons who are moved by the Spirit ACT on the presence of the Spirit within them.

Examples include:

Impetuous Peter, who denied Christ three times, and yet was chosen to lead the Church.

Ambrose, who wasn't even baptized at the time, and yet was elected bishop by the people.

Catherine of Siena, who ended the Avignon captivity of the pope by her counsel.

John XXIII, who called for Vatican II.

Anwar Sadat and Menachem Begin, who met at Camp David for peace talks.

Name two other people whom you think have been guided by the Spirit of God. What actions of their lives express the presence of the Spirit?

_____

_____

_____

_____

_____

_____

Describe a time when you have felt the presence of the Spirit in your life. How did you respond?

_____

_____

_____

_____

_____

_____

_____

_____

"The Spirit blows where it will". . . and its presence can find expression in many religions and people who seek justice and human rights for all. Unfortunately, religious differences sometimes create conflict and thwart the presence of the Spirit. Examples include the conflicts in Ireland between Catholics and Protestants and the struggles in India between Hindus and Moslems.

Research the history of one of these conflicts or another conflict in our global community that originated because of religious differences. Is religion still the primary issue? Have there been times of peace or people who tried to bring peace? What is the status of the situation today? What might help to create change? Write your thoughts on the following statement. The Spirit is inclusive; human beings are often exclusive.

_____

_____

_____

_____

_____

_____

_____

_____

_____

A recent newspaper article described the reaction of a young Protestant girl in Northern Ireland who found herself standing between two Catholics at a funeral of her friend who had been killed in a street fight. Her response was, "It is very difficult to hate people whom I know." What part does dialogue and understanding play in the work of the Spirit? How does ignorance thwart the work of the Spirit?

_____

_____

_____

_____

_____

_____

_____

_____

Marriage

Readings: **Genesis 2:18-24; Hebrews 2:9-11; Mark 10:2-16**

Listed below are qualities that enter into a marriage relationship. Choose the three that you think are **most** important. Give a brief reason for your answer. Share the list with your family, your best friend, and/or the person you're dating, and ask them to select three. Listen to their choices and their reasons. State your choices and your reasons. Can you reach a consensus on three?

share faith	*fidelity*	*physical attraction*	*common views on use of money*
communication	*trust*	*ability to forgive*	*shared hobbies/interests*
emotional maturity	*honesty*	*desire for children*	*views marriage as permanent*

There are no "right" or "wrong" answers. Hopefully, the exercise helps you to consider that two unique persons enter marriage with their individual opinions, backgrounds, and values. In marriage they are called to be one: to listen, grow, and learn together in a partnership that enhances both of their lives.

Influences on a Relationship: Jan and Mike met at a college party sponsored by Jan's sorority. They began dating occasionally and found that they enjoyed one another's company and shared some common interests.

Jan's hometown is a large city in a neighboring state. She came to the university to put some distance between herself and her family. Her father is president of the company that Jan's grandfather founded. Since Jan is an only child, her father is strongly encouraging her to seek a degree in business and return to the company.

Mike is from a small town. He is attending the university primarily on academic scholarships and loans. A part-time job provides his spending money. Mike is the oldest of four children. His mother has been their primary means of support, as Mike's dad became an alcoholic and later deserted the family.

Jan and Mike's relationship has become more serious, but they are meeting opposition from Jan's parents and no response from Mike's mother.

What factors could create future conflicts for Jan and Mike? _____

_____

How would the qualities you selected in the first exercise be nurtured in Jan and Mike's situation?

_____

What qualities from the first exercise do you see as potential areas of concern? _____

_____

What short-term and long-range impact does parental response have on a dating or marriage relationship?

_____

When is a marriage not a marriage? What is an annulment?

Divorce is a civil decree that dissolves a marriage contract. In the eyes of the state, it means putting an end to a contract in a way that protects the rights of the individuals involved.

Annulment is completely different from divorce. When the Church grants an annulment to a married couple, it is basically saying this: Despite all the outward appearance, the couple has never been sacramentally married. Therefore, in the eyes of the Church, they are not married and are free to separate from one another. They are each free to enter a sacramental marriage with another person, if that marriage meets the requirements of the Church.

To put it simply, an annulment is a judgment by the Church—after very careful study of the facts—that the couple never entered a sacramental marriage in the first place. Even though the couple went to the priest and did everything right in terms of the externals, there were hidden obstacles present that prevented the couple from actually forming a covenant relationship involving Jesus and the Church.

Here are some of the obstacles, or impediments as they are officially called, that can prevent a couple from being able to enter a sacramental marriage:

- Mental illness
- A person's hidden intention not to remain faithful, not to enter a permanent marriage, or not to be open to having children, even though he or she must make those promises
- One of the persons is already legally or sacramentally married
- Physical illness that makes it perpetually impossible to have intercourse

If any of these are present when the marriage promises are made, it blocks the sacramental marriage from taking place; there is no sacramental covenant. If the Church finds that an impediment was present when the couple made their promises, the marriage may be annulled—it decides there was no marriage. Other reasons sometimes given for annulling a marriage include the following:

- A person was psychologically unable to give a full, mature consent
- The couple did not have intercourse during their marriage
- An individual was incapable of a lifelong commitment to another person
- Lack of discretion (one or both did not understand what they were committing themselves to— sometimes the case with young couples)
- Alcoholism
- Homosexuality

The Church does not grant annulments easily. The process includes a serious investigation that tries to get all the facts as they were before the marriage and at the time the marriage took place. But the Church does give more annulments than many people realize. When a Catholic marriage does end in divorce, the couple should at least check to see if an annulment is possible. There is the chance that they were never married in the first place according to the criteria of the Church. If no annulment is granted, marriage to another partner is not allowed by the Church.

Not Ours to Judge

Any time any couple divorces, including couples in civil marriages, it is sad. People are hurt. Lives are damaged. Innocent children may suffer. It is especially tragic when the marriage was sacramental.

But divorce happens—often. Everyone knows people who are divorced: friends of the family, relatives, maybe even parents. As a result, almost everyone realizes that it is not fair to judge why a marriage fails or whether others are in sin. Divorce is tragic and not at all promoted by the Church. But this does not give anyone the right or wisdom to judge others.

Only God can probe people's hearts and know all their actions. Even the Church can only judge mostly on the externals, leaving final judgment on sinfulness to God. People who oppose divorce are still expected to respect divorced people rather than judge the state of their souls. Each person would do well to remember that God is a very merciful, forgiving God, as well as a challenging and just God. Even if there is fault present, the Lord's forgiveness is always available to be accepted through repentance. Jesus wants his followers to imitate him in the way he revealed and embodied the forgiving love of God our Father and Judge.

New Creation People by Richard Reichert from The New Creation Series (Dubuque, IA: BROWN Publishing-ROA Media, 1985), 97–98.

Make a list of qualities that a person needs in order to enter the Sacrament of Marriage. How can a person develop these qualities? _____

_____

What marriage preparation programs are required in your diocese? Talk to several couples who have recently married. Ask what they found most helpful about the program.

Searching for God

Readings: Wisdom 7:7–11; Hebrews 4:12–13; Mark 10:17–30

Millard Fuller

Even as a boy, Millard Fuller had a talent for making money. As a teenager he made enough money as a livestock trader to pay his way through college. While he was in college, he and another student made money by offering services to other students and then investing the money they made. By the time Fuller was twenty-nine, he was almost a millionaire. He kept a diary of his daily earnings and stewed if they weren't higher than the previous day's earnings.

But Millard devoted so much time to his work that his wife and his two children didn't see him much. One day Linda, his wife, left, taking their two children. Millard was crushed. He realized that although his business was flourishing, it was at the cost of his marriage, his family, and even his health. Millard took time to reevaluate his life. One day while watching a TV movie, a line from the film struck him. "A planned life can only be endured." Millard realized that his life was planned with the objective of making money. He had left out what was most important.

Millard went to New York to see his wife and their children. Together he and Linda decided to start anew. They sold everything they had and gave it away to Churches, colleges, and charities. For a time Millard worked as a fundraiser for a small college in Mississippi. Millard was happy that his family was back together again. He found his work satisfying, but he still yearned for a mission that would summon all his energy and ability.

Then, in cooperation with a Christian community in Georgia, he began to organize a project to build houses for low-income families. He organized a corporation that would build houses and sell them to families at cost. The corporation would be funded by donations, but the buyers themselves would invest time and energy in helping to construct their own house and those of their neighbors.

Eventually the project Millard started grew into an international project called *Habitat for Humanity.* Habitat's objective is to wipe out ramshackle housing worldwide. Today there are Habitat for Humanity projects in over 250 United States cities and over fifty in foreign countries. Volunteers come from the local community and from far away to work beside buyers in building projects. "I was looking for a way to measure myself in terms other than money," says one volunteer.

"You get a sense of joy in this work," says Millard, "The most dynamic people I know are concerned about something beyond themselves."

Read Mark 10:17-30. What similarities do you see between the gospel story and the story about Millard Fuller?

_____

_____

What differences do you see? _____

_____

_____

On a hot July morning in Charlotte, NC, Millard Fuller and 350 volunteer builders were working to build fourteen houses. "Who's paying for all this?" asked a passerby.

"Nobody," Millard replied.

"Folks don't do this sort of thing for nothing," the man said dubiously.

"It's worse than that," said Millard. "They paid to come. These are people from Churches around the country. They simply want to come and help."

"Man, that's real religion," said the onlooker.

Do you agree? Why or why not? _____

_____

_____

As you think about your life's work, what values will guide your choice? Look at the values listed below. Write "1" beside the value which will be most important, and number the rest of the values in order of their importance. On the line beside the value, tell why you think this is or is not a value for you.

—— I will be able to make good money.   _____

—— I like to do this kind of work.   _____

—— I am good at doing this.   _____

—— I want to help other people.   _____

—— My parents want me to do this.   _____

—— I think this is a good way to live my faith. _____

—— This is what my friends are going to do. _____

Is there a Habitat for Humanity project in your area? Is there some way you could help? To find out more about Habitat for Humanity, write to: Habitat for Humanity, Habitat and Church Streets, Box RD, Americus, GA 31709.

Story adapted from "Millard Fuller's Blueprint for Success," Reader's Digest _(June 1988): 155-159._

Twenty-Ninth Sunday
in Ordinary Time

Christians Serve

Readings: **Isaiah 53:10-11; Hebrews 4:14-16; Mark 10:35-45**

In carrying out his earthly mission as the Messiah and out of love for His Father and for us, Jesus died for us. By accepting his suffering, Jesus redeemed humankind. As followers of Christ, we are to imitate Christ by loving, healing, living as he lived. We can do this by sharing hope, courage, and healing with others who are in need.

Using the following situations, decide how your parish could respond.

1. A small town in your state is hit by a tornado. The town is destroyed and many people lose their lives.

_____

_____

_____

_____

2. Three teens are killed in a car accident on the night before their high school graduation.

_____

_____

_____

_____

3. The father of a large family is injured at work and has little chance of getting well enough to go back to work.

_____

_____

_____

_____

The Gospel according to Mark was written for a community of Christians who were suffering persecution for their faith in Jesus. Mark writes to encourage them in their faith. Christians can expect to face suffering, he seems to be saying, just as Jesus faced suffering. But Christians must serve as Jesus did, despite the suffering that may come their way. This is not an easy idea to accept, and Mark shows how long it took for the first disciples to understand what Jesus meant. They always seemed to want to change the subject and talk about something else. They foolishly debate about who will have the highest places in the kingdom.

But Mark also encourages his disciples by showing that their suffering will not go unrewarded. Jesus trusted in God throughout his life, despite his suffering and death. In the end, Jesus was vindicated in his glorious resurrection.

The Christian believer who wants to follow Jesus can expect to experience hardship and even suffering. But, like Jesus, we can trust that God will give us what we need to endure. In the end we can expect that God will triumph and we will be rewarded.

Give examples of persons who have lived out their faith despite suffering. Have they been rewarded?

_____

_____

_____

In their pastoral letter to Black Catholics in the United States, the ten bishops of the United States who are African-American, reminded their brothers and sisters in faith,

> Our own history has taught us that preaching to the poor and to those who suffer injustice without concern for their plight and the systemic cause of their plight is to trivialize the gospel and mock the cross. To preach to the powerful without denouncing oppression is to promise Easter without Calvary, forgiveness without conversion, and healing without cleansing the wound. Our concern for social justice, moreover, goes beyond denouncing injustice in the world around us. It brings us to the examination of our own hearts and intentions. It reminds us that it was the despised and rejected Samaritan who had the compassion to bind up the wounds of the other and to provide a lesson for the Chosen (see Luke 10:29–37).

"What We Have Seen and Heard," A Pastoral Letter on Evangelization from the Black Bishops of the United States, (Washington, DC: USCC, 9 September 1984): 33.

How is the suffering of oppressed groups similar to the suffering of the Suffering Servant? **Reread Isaiah 53:1–11.** Tell how one of these groups lives this passage. _____

_____

_____

Thirtieth Sunday in
Ordinary Time

Power in Weakness

Readings: **Jeremiah 31:7-9; Hebrews 5:1-6; Mark 10:46-52**

. . . the story of Jesus' adult life in three of the four Gospels is not necessarily told in chronological order, but, rather, as a single journey from his birth and hometown to the place where he was to rise again and ascend to his Father. It is, then, not a journey merely from the beginning of life to its end, but from the beginning of life to Life—everlasting and unlimited.

In his own journey from human birth to fullness of life in God, Jesus confirmed to us that only the reality of God is large enough to truly satisfy all of our dreams, and that only the power of God can help us to make them all come true. So then, our lives, and each stage of our lives, are a journey, too. They are a journey from life to Life. From a purely material and limited human existence, our lives are a searching for the unlimited fulfillment of human life in God.

Searching *by Michele McCarty (Dubuque, IA: BROWN Publishing-ROA Media, 1984), 4-5.*

The story of Jesus' life can help us to understand the story of our own lives. Today's story about the blind beggar Bartimaeus can help us to reflect on ways in which we, too, are blind and need to be healed.

Reflect on this gospel passage, **Mark 10:46-52.** How are you like Bartimaeus?

1. At the beginning of the reading, Bartimaeus is blind. When do you feel as if you cannot see? _____
_____
_____

2. Bartimaeus was a beggar. When do you feel like you are poor and have nothing to give? _____
_____
_____

3. Many people scolded Bartimaeus when he called out to Jesus. When do you feel that others keep you away from Jesus? _____
_____
_____

4. Jesus told the people to bring Bartimaeus to him. The people said to Bartimaeus, "You have nothing whatever to fear from him." How would you feel if someone told you that you had nothing whatever to fear from Jesus and that he was calling you over to be near him? _____
_____
_____

. Bartimaeus told Jesus, "I want to see." What would you tell Jesus if you met him? _____
_____
_____

6. Jesus said, "Be on your way. Your faith has saved you." Bartimaeus followed Jesus up the road. What would you do if Jesus said the same thing to you? _____
_____
_____

Draw a cartoon about some blindness you experience in the world around you. Show how it can be healed.

God's Friends

Readings: **Revelation 7:2–4, 9–14; 1 John 3:1–3; Matthew 5:1–12**

All of us have heroes and heroines. They are people who have some quality that we would like to have. They are living examples of our own personal goals.

Name someone you have had as a hero or heroine either now or earlier in your life. Why is or was this person a hero or heroine for you?

_____

_____

For centuries the Church has told stories about heroes and heroines who have done great things for God and for others. These heroes and heroines are called *saints*. Most Catholic Christians can tell some stories about saints. We place pictures of saints in places of honor in our churches and in our homes.

Name one saint whose image can be found in your parish church.

_____

What is a saint? When St. Paul wrote letters to the early Christians, he called them saints, as well as those who had "died in the Lord." Christians are saints, or holy ones, because they live in union with Christ. It is the love of God in them that makes them holy.

But very early in the history of the Church, the use of the term *saint* came to be narrowed. A saint was a person who was with God in heaven. The saint was someone who could intercede for the Church on earth. A saint was someone who was given public honor in the Church.

Until Christianity was declared legal in the fourth century, the term *saint* was almost synonymous with martyrs. Christians believed that those who had laid down their lives for their faith in Jesus were with God in heaven. They prayed to the martyrs and asked them to intercede for them in times of difficulty. They honored the martyr especially on the anniversary of the person's martyrdom.

But the veneration of saints did not die out when martyrdom was less frequent, nor did the number of saints venerated stop increasing. People looked to other Christians who lived holy lives as saints. Many lives of the saints were written to inspire others to follow the example of the saints. Christians prayed to these saints, and some claimed that God had intervened in their lives by a miracle because of the intercession of the saint. Stories of such miracles greatly increased devotion to the saint. Inevitably, fact and fiction, folklore and exaggeration crept into the stories of the saints. It is sometimes hard to determine what in the lives of the saints was true and what was pious exaggeration.

St. Christopher is popularly known to modern Catholics as the patron of motorists. Find out why and write the explanation here. Also find out why the Church no longer officially celebrates his feast day.

_____

_____

_____

For the first six or seven centuries of the Church's life, there was no formal process to recognize a person as a saint. A saint was someone who had died and who the people recognized as one who had lived an exceptionally holy life. Later, it was required that the bishop, as the pastor of the local Church, should approve devotion to a particular "saint." Still later, it was required that this official approval be given by the pope.

Why do you think the approval of the bishop or the pope was important?

_____

_____

Can you think of modern examples of people who have been misled by someone they considered holy?

_____

_____

Today the Church has a long bureaucratic process for naming a person a saint. It is called *canonization.* Canonization means that the Church believes that this saint is with God in heaven and is worthy of the honor given to saints in the Church.

Of course there are more saints in heaven than those who have been canonized. The Solemnity of All Saints is set aside to honor not only the canonized saints, but all the other saints who are with God in heaven. It is also a day to recognize that we, too, are called to be saints.

Saint Monica

114

Thirty-First Sunday in
Ordinary Time

Love of God and Love of Neighbor

Readings: **Deuteronomy 6:2-6; Hebrews 7:23-28; Mark 12:28-34**

Should Religion and Politics Mix?

"Christians should say their prayers and stay out of politics," is a criticism sometimes heard in casual conversation. It reflects the fact that the command to "Love your neighbor as yourself" can be much more controversial than the command to "Love God with your whole heart and soul and mind and strength." But Jesus is very clear. The two commands are one. Love of God shows itself in love of neighbor. To separate the two is to distort the gospel.

While loving our neighbor is not an optional part of the gospel, that does not mean that Christians can have only one approach to carrying out that command. Christians must be guided by the two great commandments in fashioning the laws and institutions of society.

But Christians may disagree on the best ways to carry out this command. So our religion has a great deal to do with our politics. It gives us the principles which guide us in our responsibilities as citizens. But in the art of politics many different needs and principles must be balanced in order to arrive at a way to ensure the common good. Ordinarily Churches and religious leaders do not spell out to their members the particular way those principles should be carried out. However, if a particular path, such as the Holocaust, clearly violates human moral principles and dignity, the Church must speak out in clear and absolute terms.

Name five political issues which currently divide Christians in the United States.

1. _____
2. _____
3. _____
4. _____
5. _____

Choose one of the issues you have named. Tell how the two great commandments apply to this issue.

_____
_____
_____

Name some other Christian principles that apply to this issue.

_____
_____
_____

Interview two adults on this issue. What solutions do they offer?

1. _____
_____
2. _____
_____

115

Evaluate the solutions offered.

• Do you think they are guided by the two great commandments? Give reasons for your answer.

1. _____

_____

2. _____

_____

• Do you think these solutions will work? Why or why not?

1. _____

_____

2. _____

_____

What solution do you think would work?

_____

_____

Are you guided by the two great commandments?

_____

_____

A Message from Pope John Paul II to American Youth

Faced with problems and disappointments, many people will try to escape from their responsibility: escape in selfishness, escape in sexual pleasure, escape in drugs, escape in violence, escape in indifference and cynical attitudes. But today I propose to you the option of love, which is really the opposite of escape.

If you really accept that love from Christ, it will lead you to God. Perhaps in the priesthood or religious life, perhaps in some special service to your brothers and sisters, especially the needy, the poor, the lonely, the abandoned, those whose rights have been trampled upon, those whose basic needs have not been provided for. Whatever you make of your own life, let it be something that reflects the love of Christ.

And when you wonder about your role in the future of the world and of the United States, look to Christ. Only in Christ will you fulfill your potential as an American citizen and as a citizen of the world community.

Taken from Origins, vol. 9: no. 17 (11 October 1979): 268–269, and Origins, vol. 9: no. 18 (18 October 1979): 296.

Pope John Paul II spoke these words to young people during his visit to the United States in 1979. How do you think these words still apply to young Americans today?

_____

_____

_____

_____

_____

_____

_____

116

Thirty-Second Sunday
in Ordinary Time

We Are Called to Share

Readings: 1 Kings 17:10-16; Hebrews 9:24-28; Mark 12:38-44

Tithing has become a way of life for the Summers family. Every month Grace Summers writes a check to the Church for 8 percent of the family's monthly income. Each month the family picks another needy person or group to whom they give another 2 percent of the family's income. "It's a family tradition," the Summers say.

"I remember when I was growing up," says Mrs. Summers. "My folks always tithed. They always said that God would not be outdone in generosity."

"It's been true for us," says George Summers, "although sometimes it seems like God is testing us."

"Once when I was in college," Tenike says, "there was a recession. My father wrote to me and told me to apply for a scholarship. He would never have thought of reducing the family's tithe."

"I always tell the children that everything we have is a gift from God," George adds. "We're just God's stewards. We have to give an account to God of how we use our time, our talents, and our possessions."

What do you think about the Summers' practice of tithing?

_____

_____

_____

_____

Tithing is an ancient practice of giving one tenth of one's income to God. The practice of tithing can be found not only in Israel but in other religions of the time. Usually the tithe was understood not as a tax, but as a sacrificial offering to God. The tithes were often made in offerings such as grain, wine, and oil. Some of these tithes were used in the sacrifices offered in worship. A part of the tithe went to care for the poor, the widows, and the orphans. Another part of the tithe was given to support the temple worship, including the Levites and priests.

Look up the following Old Testament passages about tithing. What do they add to your understanding about tithing?

Deuteronomy 26:1-15 _____

_____

Deuteronomy 14:22-29 _____

_____

2 Chronicles 31:2-10 _____

_____

Malachi 3:8-10 _____

_____

There is no law of tithing in the New Testament, but Jesus did criticize the practice of those concerned only with keeping the letter of the law perfectly. They considered the paying of the tithe as a proof of one's piety. But they extended the law of tithing to even the smallest herbs. Read the following New Testament passages. Why did Jesus criticize what some Pharisees did in these passages?

Matthew 23:23 _____

_____

Luke 18:9–14 _____

_____

Mark 10:38–40 _____

_____

The early Church had no tithing system. They relied on the generosity of Christians. Christians took very seriously Jesus' teaching about love. "See how they love one another," was a remark made about those early Christians. They also tried to imitate Jesus' care for the poor. The offerings they brought to the Sunday Eucharist included food and other items to be given to the poor. They also considered it their responsibility to support those who ministered to them. See Luke 10:7. Paul preferred to work for a living as a tentmaker, so that he could preach the gospel "free of charge." See 1 Corinthians 9:1–17.

The practice of the Church throughout history has varied. It varies in different countries today. In Christian Europe, the tithe to support the Church was often part of one's taxes. Even today in many European countries the Church and the Church's ministers are supported by taxes. In the United States, the Church has always relied on free-will offerings. Many Protestant Churches consider tithing an expected sign of commitment to the Church. The Catholic Church in the United States has never required tithing, but Catholics have always been expected to contribute to the support of the Church.

Many parishes ask their members to consider tithing their **time, talent, and treasure.** Members are asked to make a commitment to contribute a portion of their time, their talents and abilities, and their possessions to the Church and its works. What do you think about this practice? _____

_____

What guidance does today's gospel story have to offer? **Read Mark 12:38–44.** _____

_____

_____

Dedication of St. John
Lateran, November 9

Christt Dwells among Us

Readings: **Isaiah 56:1, 6-7; 1 Peter 2:4-9; John 4:19-24, or any readings from the Common of the Dedication of a Church**

What is the Church? Is the Church a who or a what? Is the Church a building or an organization? Who is the Church?

Some people think of the Church as a building where they go to worship. Others think of the Church as the pope and the bishops and priests. All of these are inadequate understandings of what the Church is. Look up the following passages from the Bible. What does the Church mean to the writer?

1 Corinthians 3:16-17 _____

_____

Ephesians 2:19-22 _____

_____

1 Peter 2:4-9 _____

_____

In the following titles of books, what does the word *church* mean?

Blueprint for a Working Church _____

_____

Authority in the Church _____

_____

The Church of the Lord _____

_____

The Church's Struggle in South America _____

_____

Puebla: Moment of Decision for the Latin American Church _____

_____

The Church is the People of God, the Body of Christ. But in order for any group of people to work together, there is a need for organization. So the Church can be considered an organization. But it is a mistake to think that the organization is just its leaders. All of us are part of the organization which is the Church.

A church building is a gathering place for the Church, in much the same way that a living room is not alive, but a place where the family lives. In order to make a living room a place that can help the family feel at ease, families decorate it according to their own tastes. We decorate a nursery in ways that will show the baby our love and delight in his or her presence. We design our kitchens in ways that will enable those who work there to both enjoy their work and serve the family's needs.

In much the same way, we design a church building in ways that will enable the Church to worship well together. We try to make our churches places where people will feel welcome. In our churches, we try to establish an environment of reverence and joy in God's presence.

How does your parish church building provide a good environment for the gathering of the Church?

_____

_____

_____

_____

What would help to make your parish church building a better environment for the gathering of the Church?

_____

_____

_____

_____

_____

_____

_____

_____

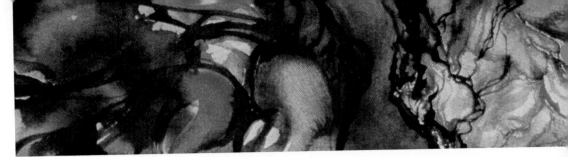

Thirty-Third Sunday in
Ordinary Time

The Lord Will Come

Readings: **Daniel 12:1-3; Hebrews 10:11-14, 18; Mark 13:24-32**

When you think about the second coming of Christ, are you more likely to have feelings of hope or of fear? Why?

_____

_____

_____

_____

Do you know anyone who thinks he or she knows when the second coming will come? On what does this person base his or her opinion?

_____

_____

_____

_____

When you look at the world today, what signs can you see that could make you think that the world will soon be coming to an end?

_____

_____

_____

_____

Throughout history, especially in times of social upheaval or chaos, people begin to look for the world to end. "How can the world go on this way?" they asked. "If it gets any worse the world will self-destruct." Christians have often found support for this position in Scripture as they interpret it. Some have predicted the exact day and time of the second coming of Christ. They have all been mistaken.

What do Catholic Christians believe about the second coming of Christ? The Catholic Church's approach to the second coming of Christ is based on the same Scriptures that fundamentalists interpret literally. However, Catholic Scripture scholars point out that these Scriptures must be read as apocalyptic, a specific kind of writing.

Apocalyptic language was very popular in Jesus' time. This manner of writing used highly symbolic language to encourage people in times of persecution and great suffering. It reminded people that it is God who is in final control of history. We must be faithful to God even in times of trial and persecution. In the end God will triumph. The good will be rewarded and evil will be punished.

In what way does apocalyptic writing encourage believers to hope?

_____

_____

_____

_____

The first generation of Christians hoped to see Christ's coming within their own lifetimes. They looked forward to this parousia with great joy. They expected to see the fulfillment of all of God's promises. They prayed, "Marana tha," "Come, Lord Jesus." Paul worked with great urgency to bring the good news throughout the civilized world because he believed that Jesus would come very soon. The Church had to learn what looking forward to the second coming could mean.

Even though we cannot name an exact time or describe the event, Christians do believe that Christ "will come to judge the living and the dead."

How do you feel when you think about this judgment?

_____

_____

_____

_____

Many people tend to think of judgment as something negative. They think of judgment as determining penalties for sins and offenses. But the judgment of Christ can also be seen in a positive way. When Christ comes, all the injustices in the world will be corrected. Christ will be a merciful judge.

For most of us, Christ's coming will be at our death. It is then that we will have our own personal judgment. If we have been open to God's love, we will be rewarded with eternal happiness. Those who have rejected God's love will find that they will be eternally separated from God in hell. For those who have not been sufficiently open to God's love, there will be purification or purgatory before they enter into the joy of heaven.

Use the information on this page to explain what is meant by each of the following words.

Heaven: _____

_____

Hell: _____

_____

Purgatory: _____

_____

Although each of us will be judged at our death, we also look forward to the day when all God's promises will be fulfilled. It is on this last day that the meaning of human history will be clear.

Define the following terms.

Particular (personal) judgment: _____

_____

General judgment: _____

_____

Jesus Christ Reigns

Readings: **Daniel 7:13–14; Revelation 1:5–8; John 18:33–37**

Images of Christ

How do Christians picture Christ? Below are pictures which show how artists have represented Christ in the past. Which picture would you caption "Christ the King"?

Which of the pictures on this page are closest to the way you picture Christ to yourself? Do you react negatively to either of these pictures? Why? Write a paragraph telling how you picture Christ and why.

_____

_____

_____

_____

_____

_____

_____

_____

_____

_____

_____

123

Of course, we have no photographs of Jesus. We have no portraits by artists who saw Jesus during his public life. The Bible tells us nothing about his appearance. Our pictures arise out of our own experience of Jesus and out of our experience with other people. We read about Jesus' ministry of healing, and we remember other people who have been kind and compassionate. We read that Christ will come to judge, and we think of others who have judged us—parents, teachers, principals, or other authorities. Often we don't realize that we are creating our own images of Jesus.

Look at the pictures of Jesus in your home, in books, and in your church. Does the Jesus pictured there look like a first century Jew or does he look more like a European?

Our images of Jesus and of God are very important, however. The way we picture Jesus as strong or weak, distant or close, accepting or intolerant can make a difference in the way we relate to God and to one another. How do we know if our images of God or Jesus are good or not? For Christians, it is the Bible which serves as a norm to help us judge the adequacy of our images.

The biblical writers seemed to have a need to use many different images to talk about God. Each image gives a partial insight into what God is like. Each image gives us an understanding of one facet of the mystery that God is. Even if we put all the images together, however, we would not have a complete image of God. God is a mystery who cannot ever be completely understood. Sometimes people tend to focus on only one image of God and forget that the image is only an image. This can be a kind of idolatry. We need to always remember that God is far beyond our ability to comprehend. All our images are necessary, but each image gives only a partial insight.

The image of God as king can be found often in the Bible. Jesus talked often about the kingdom of God. But the Gospels tell us that Jesus was not at all interested in being called a king. He did not want to be identified by the image of king that the people seemed to have. He often told the people he healed to keep it a secret. After he fed the five thousand with bread, he hid himself because they wanted to make him king. As he stood before Pilate, Jesus seemed to sidestep the issue and insisted that his kingdom is different than the kinds of kingdoms they knew.

Every image of God gives us a partial insight into God. However, any image carried to its extreme or held exclusively can distort the Christian faith. Think about the image of Christ as king. Name two positive aspects of the image and two negative aspects of the image.

Positive   Negative

1. _____   _____

2. _____   _____

The Solemnity of Christ the King was established by Pope Pius XI in 1925. It was a time when Catholics and other Christians were being persecuted in Russia and in Mexico. Pope Pius XI was encouraging Catholics everywhere to build a new society based on the teachings of Christ. What value do you see in celebrating the feast today?

_____

_____

_____

_____

_____

Appendix

Sign of the Cross

In the name of the Father,
and of the Son,
and of the Holy Spirit. Amen.

The Lord's Prayer

Our Father, who are in heaven,
hallowed be Your name;
Your kingdom come;
Your will be done on earth
as it is in heaven.
Give us this day our daily bread;
and forgive us our trespasses
as we forgive those
who trespass against us;
and lead us not into temptation,
but deliver us from evil. Amen.

Hail Mary

Hail, Mary, full of grace,
the Lord is with you!
Blessed are you among women,
and blessed is the fruit
of your womb, Jesus.
Holy Mary, Mother of God,
pray for us sinners,
now and at the hour of our death. Amen.

Trinity Prayer

Glory to the Father,
and to the Son,
and to the Holy Spirit.
As it was in the beginning,
is now, and will be forever. Amen.

Act of Contrition

O my God, I am sorry for my sins.
In choosing to sin,
and failing to do good,
I have sinned against You and Your Church.
I firmly intend,
with the help of Your son,
to do penance and to sin no more.
Our Savior Jesus Christ
suffered and died for us.
In his name, my God, have mercy.

Grace before Meals

Bless us, O Lord, and these Your gifts,
which we are about to receive from Your bounty,
through Christ our Lord. Amen.

Morning Offering

God, my Father, I give You today,
All that I think and do and say.
And I unite with all that was done
By Jesus Christ, Your dearest Son.

Apostles' Creed

I[We] believe in God,
the Father almighty,
creator of heaven and earth.
I[We] believe in Jesus Christ,
His only Son, our Lord.
He was conceived by the power of the Holy Spirit
and born of the Virgin Mary.
He suffered under Pontius Pilate,
was crucified, died, and was buried.
He descended to the dead.
On the third day He rose again.
He ascended into heaven,
and is seated at the right hand of the Father.
He will come again to judge
the living and the dead.
I[We] believe in the Holy Spirit,
the holy catholic Church,
the communion of saints,
the forgiveness of sins,
the resurrection of the body,
and life everlasting. Amen.

Memorare

Remember, O most loving Virgin Mary,
that never was it known
That anyone who fled to your protection,
implored your help,
or sought your intercession
was left unaided.
Inspired with this confidence, we turn to you,
O Virgin of Virgins, our Mother.
To you we come, before you we kneel,
sinful and sorrowful.
O Mother of the Word Incarnate,
do not despise our petitions,
but in your mercy hear and answer us. Amen.

St. Bernard

The Laws of the Church

1. To keep Sundays holy, and to participate in Mass on Sundays and holy days of obligation.
2. To lead a sacramental life, frequently receiving the Eucharist.
3. To prepare for Confirmation and to be confirmed.
4. To observe the marriage laws of the Church and to provide children with religious training.
5. To strengthen and support the Church.
6. To do penance, including abstaining from meat and fasting from food on appointed days.
7. To join in the missionary spirit and the works of the Church.

The Ten Commandments

1. I, the Lord, am your God. You shall not have other gods beside me.
2. You shall not take the name of the Lord, your God, in vain.
3. Remember to keep holy the Sabbath Day.
4. Honor your father and your mother.
5. You shall not kill.
6. You shall not commit adultery.
7. You shall not steal.
8. You shall not bear false witness against your neighbor.
9. You shall not covet your neighbor's wife.
10. You shall not covet anything that belongs to your neighbor.

The Beatitudes

Happy are those who know they are spiritually poor; the kingdom of heaven belongs to them.

[Happy the gentle; they shall have the earth as their heritage.]

Happy are those who mourn; God will comfort them.

Happy are those who are humble; they will receive what God has promised.

Happy are those whose greatest desire is to do what God requires; God will satisfy them fully.

Happy are those who are merciful to others; God will be merciful to them.

Happy are the pure in heart; they shall see God.

Happy are those who work for peace; God will call them His children.

Happy are those who are persecuted because they do what God requires; the kingdom of heaven belongs to them.

Prayer to the Holy Spirit

Come, Holy Spirit, fill the hearts of Your faithful and enkindle in them the fire of Your love. Send forth Your Spirit and they shall be created. And You shall renew the face of the earth.

O God, who instructs the hearts of the faithful by the light of the Holy Spirit, grant us by the same Holy Spirit to love what is right and ever to rejoice in His consolation through Christ our Lord.

The Rosary

The Joyful Mysteries (Mondays and Thursdays)

1. Annunciation
2. The Visitation
3. The Birth of Jesus
4. The Presentation in the Temple
5. Mary and Joseph Find Jesus in the Temple.

The Sorrowful Mysteries (Tuesdays and Fridays)

1. The Agony in the Garden
2. The Scourging of Jesus
3. The Crowning with Thorns
4. Jesus Carries His Cross
5. Jesus Dies on the Cross

The Glorious Mysteries (Sundays, Wednesdays, and Saturdays)

1. The Resurrection
2. The Ascension
3. The Holy Spirit Is Sent upon the Apostles
4. The Assumption of Mary
5. Mary Is Crowned Queen of Heaven and Earth

Spiritual Works of Mercy

Warn the sinner.

Instruct the ignorant.

Counsel the doubtful.

Comfort the sorrowing.

Be patient with those who hurt you.

Pray for the living and the dead.

Forgive injuries.

Corporal Works of Mercy

Feed the hungry.

Give drink to the thirsty.

Clothe the naked.

Visit the imprisoned.

Shelter the homeless.

Visit the sick.

Bury the dead.

Holy Days of Obligation

In the United States, the following holy days of obligation are observed.

Christmas (December 25)

The Solemnity of Mary Mother of God (January 1)

Ascension Thursday (fortieth day after Easter)

Assumption of Mary (August 15)

All Saints (November 1)

Immaculate Conception (December 8)

The Angelus

V. The angel spoke God's message to Mary,

R. and she conceived of the Holy Spirit.

Hail, Mary . . . .

V. "I am the lowly servant of the Lord:

R. let it be done to me according to Your word."

Hail, Mary. . . .

V. And the Word became flesh

R. and lived among us.

Hail, Mary. . . .

V. Pray for us, holy Mother of God,

R. that we may become worthy of the promises of Christ.

Let us pray.

Lord, fill our hearts with your grace:
once, through the message of an angel,
You revealed to us the incarnation of your Son;
now, through His suffering and death,
lead us to the glory of His resurrection.
We ask this through Christ our Lord.

R. Amen.

Taken from Household Blessings and Prayers

(Washington, DC: USCC, 1988), 363-364.

Examination of Conscience

We prepare for the Sacrament of Reconciliation by thinking about how we live Jesus' Law of Love. These questions can help us think about our lives.

How did I show my love for God and others?

Did I pray?

Did I listen to and obey my parents?

Did I think of others? My parents? My brothers and sisters? Was I considerate of them?

My teacher and friends? Was I kind to them?

Was I kind and fair in work and recreation?

Did I share?

Did I care for my possessions? For those of others?

Did I hurt others by lying or stealing or name calling?

Did I worship God by going to Mass and taking part in the celebration?

Celebrating the Sacrament of Forgiveness

1. The priest welcomes you and prays for you.
2. The priest may read a passage from Scripture.
3. You tell the priest your sins. He talks to you about Jesus' Law of Love.
4. The priest gives you a penance.
5. You then say the Act of Contrition.
6. The priest extends his hands over you and says: "I absolve you from your sins, in the name of the Father, and of the Son, ✠ and of the Holy Spirit."
7. The priest then tells you to go in peace, and you answer: Amen.

Rogation Days

The Rogation Days were traditionally celebrated on the three days before the solemnity of the Ascension. They may now be celebrated at any time when it is appropriate to ask that gardens, fields, and orchards be blessed during the coming season. The blessing takes place in the midst of the garden or field.

> *O God,*
> *from the very beginning of time*
> *you commanded the earth to bring forth vegetation*
> *and fruit of every kind.*
> *You provide the sower with seed and give bread to eat.*
> *Grant, we pray, that this land,*
> *enriched by your bounty and cultivated by human hands,*
> *may be fertile with abundant crops.*
> *Then your people, enriched by the gifts of your goodness,*
> *will praise you unceasingly now and for ages unending.*
> *Grant this through Christ our Lord. Amen.*

The above explanation and prayer are taken from Household Blessings and Prayers *(Washington, DC: USCC, 1988); an entire prayer service/blessing can be found on pages 166–169 of that book.*

Answers

Second Sunday of Advent

Liturgical Year
Dec. 2, 1990
Mar. 31, 1991
Feb. 13, 1991
May 19, 1991
Dec. 2, 1990–Dec. 24, 1990
Dec. 25, 1990–Jan. 13, 1991
Feb. 13, 1991–Mar. 28, 1991
Mar. 28, 1991–Mar. 31, 1991
Apr. 7, 1991–May 19,, 1991
Jan. 20, 1991–Feb. 10, 1991
June 9, 1991–Nov. 3, 1991

Liturgical Year
Nov. 28, 1993
Apr. 3, 1994
Feb. 16, 1994
May 22, 1994
Nov. 28, 1993–Dec. 24, 1993
Dec. 25, 1993–Jan. 9, 1994
Feb. 16, 1994–Mar. 31, 1994
Mar. 31, 1994–Apr. 3, 1994
Apr. 10, 1994–May 22, 1994
Jan. 16, 1994–Feb. 13, 1994
June 12, 1994–Oct. 30, 1994

Liturgical Year
Dec. 1, 1996
Mar. 30, 1997
Feb. 12, 1997
May 18, 1997
Dec. 1, 1996–Dec. 24, 1996
Dec. 25, 1996–Mar. 27, 1997
Mar. 27, 1997–Mar. 30, 1997
Apr. 6, 1997–May 18, 1997
Jan. 19, 1997–Feb. 9, 1997
June 8, 1997–Oct. 26, 1997

Fourth Sunday of Advent

The Joyful Mysteries

1. Luke 1:26–38
2. Luke 1:39–56
3. Luke 2:1–19, Matthew 1:18–25
4. Luke 2:22–40
5. Luke 2:41–52

Presentation of the Lord

Genesis 18:1–15   Abraham, three men
Exodus 33:7–11   Moses, the cloud

Simeon and Anna recognized him.
Because he is an ordinary baby.

Seventh Sunday in Ordinary Time

1. Through the Sacrament of Anointing, the Church supports the sick in their struggle against illness and continues Christ's messianic work of healing.
2. Those who are with the one being anointed.
3. Members of the family and other representatives of the Christian community. Then the sacrament is seen as a part of the prayer of the Church and as an encounter with the Lord.

Ninth Sunday in Ordinary Time

1 Corinthians 11:23–34   Since the night of the Last Supper.
1 Corinthians 11:22–25   "Do this in memory of me."

Violations of Jewish law: pulling off heads of grain on the Sabbath.
Sabbath observance: The Sabbath was made for man, not man for the Sabbath.

Fourth Sunday of Lent

The Lord told him to.
Anyone who had been bitten by serpents.
He was raised up; he saves people.
We are saved; all who believe in him.

Fifth Sunday of Lent

a, d, c, c, b

Fourth Sunday of Easter

Ezekiel 34:1–16
The shepherds have taken care of themselves. They fed off their milk, wore their wool, and slaughtered the fatlings.
I will claim my sheep, I will save my sheep.

Ezekiel 34:17–24
They trampled on the grazing area, and fouled the water with their feet.
He will save His sheep, put one shepherd over them, and be their God.

Isaiah 40:9–11
He will gather them in his arms and carry them in his bosom.

John 10:11–18
The poor shepherds are paid and so have no concern for the sheep.
Those that do not belong to the fold. He is possessed by a devil—out of his mind.

Sixth Sunday of Easter

Matching: 2, 1, 4, 3, 5, 7, 6

Seventh Sunday of Easter

120
Mary, apostles, other followers of Jesus
twelve tribes, and "May another take his office."
Whether or not Gentile converts had to keep the
Jewish laws (circumcision, food)
They agreed to not require those things and wrote
a letter to the communities.
Preaching, teaching, worship, prayer, healing,
living as a community, spreading the good news

Pentecost

2, 7, 1, 5, 6, 4, 3

Corpus Christi

Eat it.
Blood was a sign of life. (2 questions)
God was sharing His life with them through the
  covenant.

Sts. Peter and Paul

Paul's teaching came as a revelation from Christ.
False claimants to the title of brother.
He thought Peter was wrong.
They were all entrusted with the gospel and were
  the pillars of the Christian community.

Eighteenth Sunday in Ordinary Time

1. Luke 19:1–10
2. Luke 16:19–31
3. Luke 10:38–42 (The men generally talked over
   religion with the rabbi and the women served
   them. Here Jesus is giving Mary permission to
   take on this role.)
4. Luke 14:15–24
5. Luke 15:11–31
6. Luke 14:1–11